THE ROMANTIC THEATRE

THE ROMANTIC THEATRE
AN INTERNATIONAL SYMPOSIUM

edited
by
Richard Allen Cave

COLIN SMYTHE
Gerrards Cross, Bucks.

BARNES AND NOBLE BOOKS
Totowa, New Jersey

Copyright © 1986 by Sir Joseph Cheyne, Timothy Webb,
Giorgio Melchiori, Stuart Curran, and Richard Allen Cave

All rights reserved

First published in 1986 by Colin Smythe Limited
Gerrards Cross, Buckinghamshire

British Library Cataloguing in Publication Data

The Romantic Theatre: an international symposium
  1. English drama—18th century—History and criticism
  2. English drama—19th century—History and criticism.
  3. Romanticism.
  I. Cave, Richard Allen
882'.7'09   PR721
                ISBN 0-86140-238-3

First published in the United States of America in 1987
by Barnes & Noble Books, Totowa, N.J. 07512

ISBN 0-389-20697-0

Produced in Great Britain
set by Crypticks, Leeds and printed
and bound by Billing & Sons Ltd., Worcester

CONTENTS

Foreword by Sir Joseph Cheyne   7

One:
THE ROMANTIC POET AND THE STAGE: A SHORT, SAD HISTORY. Professor Timothy Webb (University of York, England)   9

Two:
THE DRAMAS OF BYRON. Professor Giorgio Melchiori (University of Rome, Italy)   47

Three:
SHELLEYAN DRAMA. Professor Stuart Curran (University of Pennsylvania, Philadelphia, America)   61

Four:
ROMANTIC DRAMA IN PERFORMANCE. Dr Richard Allen Cave (University of London, England)   79

NOTES   105

THE ROMANTICS AND THE THEATRE: A SHORT BIBLIOGRAPHY. Christina Gee and Judith Knight   113

INDEX   127

FOREWORD

In the winter of 1980-81, the Keats-Shelley Memorial Association organised in Rome, in conjunction with the British Council and the Italian authorities, an Exhibition 'The English Romantic Poets and Italy', which was held in Palazzo Braschi (kindly loaned by the Rome Town Council) and remained open for over two months. The success of the Exhibition was such that a lecture series was held at the British Council during the winter of 1981-82 to develop the same subject.

These two events engendered much interest in the Younger Romantics, especially among Italian schools, so that the Association decided to hold a further series of four lectures in the spring of 1985, again in conjunction with the British Council, and with the financial support of Barclays Bank Group in Italy. To both of these bodies, the Association expresses its gratitude.

The title of the series, 'The Romantic Theatre', was chosen partly because this was a subject which had received comparatively little study in Italy and partly because there was a growing interest among undergraduate groups to present productions or readings of the plays of Shelley and Byron.

No one realised, when the series was planned, what a remarkable impact it would have. The accepted idea of the Romantic theatre was still one of lyric drama, difficult to produce and perform. To hear it described suddenly as modern, psychological drama, as the theatre of the mind, the 'theatre of violence', was so striking that the ripples are still washing the shore.

The lectures were delivered at the British Council in Rome in April and May 1985 to a large international audience. One of the lecturers, Professor Melchiori, chose to give his lecture the character more of a talk than a formal dissertation and his contribution is reproduced here as originally given; the other speakers gave formal lectures. All four admitted their astonishment at having had (drastically) to revise their views on the Romantic drama when they came to reshape earlier material. Thus all the lectures have a rare freshness and spontaneity to colour the seriousness of their scholarly approach.

The international character and eminence of the lecturers would alone make these lectures memorable and their study essential. But it is this special vitality and novelty which must appeal also to a wide public. For these lectures throw new light not only on the Romantic theatre but also on the theatre in general. They are more than just another stage in the Romantic revival and in modern Romantic criticism. They point to the future.

The Association would like to express particular thanks to Dr. Richard Cave for his scrupulous editing of the volume; to Mrs. Christina Gee, Curator of the Keats House in Hampstead, for supervising the compilation of the Bibliography; and to Mr. Colin Smythe whose involvement in the whole project far exceeded what one normally expects of a publisher.

Sir Joseph Chene, Bart., O.B.E.
(Curator: Keats-Shelley Memorial House, Rome)

ONE:
THE ROMANTIC POET AND THE STAGE: A SHORT, SAD, HISTORY

Timothy Webb

What encouragement has a man of Education and the feelings of a Gentleman to write either Comedy or Tragedy for Drury Lane?
S. T. Coleridge

... it is indisputable that the highest perfection of human society has ever corresponded with the highest dramatic excellence; and that the corruption or the extinction of the drama in a nation where it has once flourished, is a mark of a corruption of manners, and an extinction of the energies which sustain the soul of social life. *P. B. Shelley*

I am acquainted with no *im*material sensuality so delightful as good acting ... *Lord Byron*

The age we live in is critical, didactic, paradoxical, romantic, but it is not dramatic. *William Hazlitt*[1]

Yeats once accused Wordsworth of being 'flat and heavy, partly because his moral sense has no theatrical element'.[2] Writing in 1820 Hazlitt had expressed a view which was not dissimilar:

He is not, like Bottom, ready to play the lady, the lover, and the lion. His poetry is a virtual proscription passed upon the promiscuous nature of the drama. He sees nothing but himself in the universe ... He has none of the bye-play, the varying points of view, the venturous magnanimity of dramatic fiction. . . . he thinks the 'daily intercourse of all this unintelligible world,' its cares, its crimes, its noise, love, war, ambition (what else?), mere vanity and vexation of spirit, with which a great poet cannot condescend to disturb the bright, serene, and solemn current of his thoughts.[3]

Wordsworth may be an extreme case but in many ways he seems to embody an archetype of the Romantic poet; the recognizable outlines can be traced in the self-reflexive quality of his verse, the grounding of his imaginative life in experience which is deeply personal, and his limited ability to burst through the circumference of self to an engagement with the identities of others. Of course, this pattern cannot be made to fit all of his poetic contemporaries, whether of his own generation or the next. And yet it must be admitted that the tendencies of Romantic poetry did lead towards an expression of self rather than the world, or perhaps of self in relation to the world; the Romantics were ventriloquists rather than chameleons.

Writing with full self-consciousness as one of 'the last Romantics', Yeats recognized the problem which he had inherited. In the Journal which he was keeping in 1909 and where he recorded the judgement on Wordsworth he went on to register a poetic ideal, an antidote to the tendencies of modern society which were inimical to art: 'All my life I have been haunted with the idea that the poet should know all classes of men as one of themselves, that he should combine the greatest possible personal realization with the greatest possible knowledge of the speech and circumstance of the world. Fifteen or twenty years ago I remember longing, with this purpose, to disguise myself as a peasant and wander through the West, and then shipping as a sailor.' He acknowledged the pressures which made it essential to embark on such a circuitous rediscovery of the external world and which also made it so difficult, so precariously artificial. 'The artist grows more and more distinct, more and more a being in his own right, as it were, but more and more loses grasp of the always more complex world.'[4] Yeats's struggle is suggestive both because it arises out of a heightening of the Romantic dilemma and because it helps to indicate what the Romantic tradition did not have to offer. One cannot easily imagine any of the Romantic poets aspiring to 'the greatest possible knowledge of the speech and circumstances of the world' — with the possible exception of Byron, and even he would hardly have considered the aesthetic discipline of disguising himself as a peasant or a sailor. The Romantic poets tended to work through concentration rather than through a celebration of diversity or heterogeneity; certainly, they did not accommodate themselves to the range of character which is essential to the great traditions of the English drama. The focusing of their energies is most clearly represented by Wordsworth whose great strength (as Coleridge realized) was his 'Unity of Interest, & that Homogeneity of character which is the natural consequence of it'.[5] They were neither 'hominiscien[t]' nor 'myriad-minded' as Shakespeare was according to Coleridge, 'darting himself forth, & passing into all the forms of human character & passion'.[6] They resisted the plurality of human character and behaviour just as, in Hazlitt's phrase, they passed a proscription upon the 'promiscuous nature of the drama'.

And yet, in spite of all these negatives and these unpromising reservations, the work of most of the major Romantic poets shows strong and unmistakeable tendencies towards the dramatic. Yeats's comment on Wordsworth acutely diagnoses a lack of the 'theatrical' but it does not allow for his use of the 'dramatic'. Yeats is right to sense a certain flatness which is partly the result of Wordsworth's failure to project himself outwards or to seek for the Yeatsian ideal of the mask or the anti-self, yet the sweeping condemnation does less than justice to Wordsworth's initiatory enterprise in exploring 'the Mind of Man' or, what might be called, 'the theatre of the mind'.[7] The success of a poem such as 'Resolution and Independence' depends on the poet's ability to involve us directly in his experience and to present a version of his experiencing self with a detachment which allows for the self-critical almost to the point of comedy. 'The Thorn' might be regarded as an experiment (not entirely successful) with a persona. Coleridge may have been thinking of poems like this when he pronounced that Wordsworth had 'an undue predilection for the *dramatic* form', which he regarded as an unfortunate aberration from the true source of his poetic strength.[8] Much of *The Prelude* is perhaps too reflective to satisfy the claims of the dramatic but there is an intensity of introspection and an acute responsiveness to tension and to conflict which animates many of its greatest passages; for instance, the poet thinking of the September Massacres in his lonely hotel room and hearing a voice which cries to the whole city, 'Sleep no more' or remembering 'long orations which in dreams I pleaded / Before unjust tribunals, with a voice / Labouring, a brain confounded, and a sense, / Of treachery and desertion in the place / The holiest that I knew of, my own soul'.[9] According to Wordsworth, his play *The Borderers* was also directly inspired by his first-hand observation of the changes through which the French Revolution passed: 'The study of human nature suggests this awful truth, that, as in the trials to which life subjects us, sin and crime are apt to start from their very opposite qualities, so are there no limits to the hardening of the heart, and the perversion of the understanding to which they may carry their slaves.' The evidence of the play itself suggests that it is less a commentary on the politics of revolutionary France than the result of an excursion into the deeps of the mind, an investigation of 'those tendencies of human nature which make the apparently *motiveless* actions of bad men intelligible to careful observers.'[10] Its particular interest here is that the impulses which led Wordsworth to compose his play and to write certain passages of *The Prelude* are not so diverse as one might at first imagine. That very scope and tendency of Wordsworth's mind which Hazlitt branded as 'the reverse of dramatic',[11] that 'Homogeneity' noticed by Coleridge, represented a serious obstacle to conventional dramatic achievement but it was also the locus of a particular power.

If the central Wordsworthian impulse was to record the dynamics of a drama which was acted out in his own mind and soul, the other Romantic poets performed a variety of roles in their own theatres of the imagination. The Byronic hero stamps his authority on many of Byron's poems, notably the Turkish Tales and *Childe Harold*: he is rebel, outlaw, melancholy wanderer and alienated hero, and his performances resonate with echoes of Hamlet, Faust, Cain, the Wandering Jew and Satan. More obviously still, the eponymous heroes of *Manfred* and *Cain* explore the darker reaches of human experience, proceed precariously but defiantly along the dangerous edge with a self-regarding sublimity which veers between the dramatic and the melodramatic. As G. Wilson Knight has demonstrated in convincing detail, Byron characteristically employs a Shakespearean frame of reference both in his published works and in the letters and journals where he reflects on his life, recreates it and turns it into a continuous, brilliantly sustained and highly calculated act of self-dramatization.[12]

Other, less striking, examples can be found in the life and works of Coleridge, Shelley and Keats. The cases of Wordsworth and Byron suggest that, in varying degrees, the dramatic tendency was important to the Romantic poets but that its central energies were derived from an engagement not so much with the external world as with the rich diversities and complexities of self. They were self-dramatizing rather than dramatizing. Thus Yeats and Hazlitt are essentially accurate in their diagnoses of a condition which is focused on the inner rather than the outer; and yet they have failed to register the centrality of the dramatic impulse and the consistency with which a number of the Romantic poets engaged with its possibilities.

All the major poets wrote plays, and several used dramatic form to explore some of the predominant concerns of their creativity. This applies especially to Byron and Shelley but it also has some relevance to the earlier generation. An outline of this dramatic activity might be instructive and perhaps surprising. The early work of Blake included the uncompleted *Edward the Third*, a historical drama in the Shakespearean mode which was published in *Poetical Sketches* (1783), and *An Island in the Moon* (c. 1784-5), a satirical account of fashions in contemporary intellectual life which is largely made up of dialogues and songs that pastiche and parody a variety of modes, literary, musical and theatrical. Otherwise Blake seems to have had no direct interest either in drama or in the theatre. Wordsworth, as we have seen, was the author of *The Borderers*. By his own account he did not originally intend it for the stage, although he was encouraged to submit it to Covent Garden when it was finished in 1796:

For myself, I had no hope nor even a wish (tho' a successful play would, in the then state of my finances, have been a most welcome piece of good fortune) that he should accept my performance; so that I incurred no disappointment when the piece was *judiciously* returned as not calculated for the Stage. In this judgement I entirely concurred, and had it been otherwise, it was so natural for me to shrink from public notice, that any hope I might have had of success would not have reconciled me altogether to such an exhibition.[13]

This retrospective account suggests both a lack of interest in theatrical success and a fatalistic resignation to failure which seem to be at variance with the tone of letters from Wordsworth and Dorothy before the play was rejected. Thereafter Wordsworth seems to have remained untempted by the possibilities of financial success in the theatre and uninterested in the drama as a literary form. The French Revolution also provided inspiration for Coleridge who, together with Southey, wrote *The Fall of Robespierre* (1794), an historical drama in which, as Coleridge said, 'it has been my sole aim to imitate the empassioned and highly figurative language of the French orators, and to develope 'the characters of the chief actors on a vast stage of horrors.'[14] Here Coleridge explores for dramatic purposes the theatricality of the 'monstrous tragic-comic scene' which had been so brilliantly evoked by Edmund Burke in *Reflections on the Revolution in France* (1790); not only had Burke provided a vividly critical account of the theatre of revolution but he had also achieved, as Thomas Paine pointed out, 'a dramatic performance' of his own in which he had made 'the whole machinery bend to produce a stage effect'.[15] Coleridge also translated Schiller's *The Piccolomini* and *The Death of Wallenstein* in 1800; he admitted that these plays might be disappointing to those who knew *The Robbers, Cabal and Love*, 'plays in which the main interest is produced by the excitement of curiosity, and in which the curiosity is excited by terrible and extraordinary incident' but directed such readers to the analogy not of *Lear* or *Othello* but of *Richard II* and *Henry VI*.[16] His own play *Osorio* was sent to Drury Lane in October 1797 and rejected, according to Coleridge, because of Sheridan's '*sole* objection' to the 'obscurity of the three last acts'.[17] Even before it was rejected Coleridge had exhibited a severe disillusionment with the painful business of writing plays:

In truth, I have fagged so long at the work, & seen so many imperfections in the original & main plot, that I feel an indescribable disgust, a sickness of the very heart, at the mention of the Tragedy . . . . — Excepting for the money which would be gained if it succeeded, I am not conscious of a wish relating to the piece. It is done: and I would rather mend hedges & follow the plough, than write another. I could not avoid attaching a pecuniary importance to the business; and consequently, became anxious: and such anxieties humble & degrade the mind.[18]

In spite of such anxieties and reservations, *Osorio* was eventually transformed into *Remorse*, in which shape it received twenty performances at Drury Lane in 1813. During rehearsal the play had been heavily revised and altered. Coleridge thought the continuous process of alteration was a 'tedious business' but he acknowledged that 'many of the Omissions have improved the piece no less as a dramatic Poem than as an acting Tragedy'.[19] He even pleaded for further cuts: 'it was somewhat odd, as the world goes, to have the Writer pleading strenuously for more & more excisions, and the Actors (& in one or two instances the Manager) arguing for their retention'.[20] Such eagerness to learn about 'Stage-tactics',[21] to profit from professional advice, and to submerge the proverbial vanity of the playwright earned him the compliments of the Green Room where, by his own account, he was variously known as 'the amenable Author' or 'the anomalous Author, from my utter indifference or prompt facility in sanctioning every omission that was suggested'.[22] *Remorse* was revived in 1817. *Zapolya* (1815), an imitation of *The Winter's Tale* which Coleridge described as 'a dramatic Entertainment',[23] was first rejected by Covent Garden and then sent to Drury Lane with the encouragement of Byron, only to be circuitously rejected in 1816. Coleridge recorded: 'I was informed that it would not do as a Play; but that it would answer very well as a Melodrama with some slight alteration. That this slight alteration consisted in omitting all that was of any value in the Piece did not give me a moment's concern'.[24] In this case the amenable author was not permitted to demonstrate his well-practised authorial flexibility. It seems that he was neither consulted nor remunerated when the play was altered by Dibdin and produced as a melodrama at the Royal Circus and Surrey Theatre in November of the following year. As we shall see, Coleridge also envisaged or planned a variety of rather surprising theatrical projects, all of which proved abortive.

Byron's dramatic output was largely the product of a short period of concentrated activity. His metaphysical play *Manfred* (1817) includes a striking final scene in which the pattern of *Doctor Faustus* is implicitly challenged when the hero refuses to acknowledge the jurisdiction of the evil spirits who have come to take him away; he tells them that the mind is its own place and makes itself requital for its good and evil deeds. A mysterious and unexplained aura of guilt hangs over the play which helps to give it a Gothic flavouring but which also suggests that Manfred is another variation in the line of Byronic heroes who give expression to the more troubled aspects of their creator's psychology.

Cain (1821) is a Biblical drama which also examines the question of guilt and the problem of evil. That same year Byron wrote *Heaven and Earth* and three historical plays which were concerned with questions of power and political responsibility — *Marino Faliero* and *The Two Foscari*, which were based on the history of Venice and *Sardanapalus*, which was based on the history of the last king of Assyria. Also that year he completed the melodramatic *Werner*, which was based on a story by Harriet Lee and which he had originally intended for Drury Lane. At his death he left unfinished *The Deformed Transformed* which owed debts to Joshua Pickersgill's *The Three Brothers* and to Goethe's *Faust*. Of these eight plays only *Marino Faliero* was given a performance during Byron's life; this was at Drury Lane in 1820, where it ran for seven nights in a version which was heavily edited and censored by the theatre and in spite of the fact that Byron had tried to take out an injunction against the performance. Four other plays were performed during the 1830s.[25]

Shelley claimed to have little dramatic ability but this did not prevent him from making frequent experiments: 'you will say, I have no dramatic talent. Very true in a certain sense; but I have taken the resolution to see what kind of a tragedy a person without dramatic talent could write'.[26] Shelley's plays included *Prometheus Unbound* (1820) and *Hellas* (1821), both of which he classified as 'lyrical drama', a term which may owe something to a French description of *Don Giovanni*; *Prometheus Unbound* in particular seems to owe a considerable debt to operatic models as well as to masque and, more obviously, to its Aeschylean prototype. Its exploration of musical analogies and its use of strategies and structures from opera and ballet extend the boundaries of dramatic form; Bernard Shaw acknowledged something of this when he wrote that '*Prometheus Unbound* is an English attempt at a Ring'.[27] Yet for all its expressiveness, *Prometheus Unbound* was never intended to be performed. *The Cenci*, on the other hand, was different: according to Shelley, it was not one of his 'visions which impersonate my own apprehensions of the beautiful and the just' but 'a sad reality' based on a story which was 'well known in Italy, & in my conception eminently dramatic'. Unlike *Prometheus Unbound* it was intended 'for the multitude', it was 'expressly written for theatrical exhibition' and, in Shelley's view, it was 'singularly fitted for the stage'. Shelley confessed that he was 'exceedingly interested' to see whether it succeeded; he founded his hopes on the belief that 'as a composition it is certainly not inferior to any of the modern plays that have been acted, with the exception of Remorse, that the interest of its plot is incredibly greater & more real, & that there is nothing beyond what the multitude are contented to believe that they can understand, either in imagery opinion or sentiment'. He told Peacock that 'in all respects it is fitted only for Covent Garden' and asked him to arrange for its presentation with Eliza O'Neill as Beatrice ('God forbid that I shd. see her play it — it wd. tear my nerves to pieces'). His identity was to remain a secret, unless and until the play was acted successfully (both Holcroft and Godwin had employed a similar strategy some years before). Shelley was hurt when, as he put it, 'the very Theatre rejected it with expressions of the greatest insolence', although, according to Mary Shelley, the manager 'expressed his desire that he would write a tragedy on some other subject, which he would gladly accept'. He had miscalculated the impact of the theme of incest (the manager could not even bring himself to ask Eliza O'Neill to read the part of Beatrice), having convinced himself that it ought to be acceptable both because the facts were 'matter of history' and because of 'the peculiar delicacy' with which he had treated the subject. He later criticized the 'squeamishness' which had motivated this rejection and which was 'the produce, as I firmly believe, of a *lower tone* of the *public mind*, and foreign to the *majestic and confident wisdom* of the golden age of our country'.[28]

Shelley's other plays were the political satire *Oedipus Tyrannus or Swellfoot the Tyrant* (1820) which was inspired by George IV's attempt to divorce his wife and which was confiscated and burnt after the sale of only seven copies; the fragmentary *Charles the First* which was to be written 'in the spirit of human nature, without prejudice or passion';[29] and 'Fragments of an Unfinished Drama' which, according to his wife, was 'undertaken for the amusement of the individuals who composed our intimate society'.[30] He also translated Euripides' satyr-play *The Cyclops* and scenes from Goethe's *Faust* and Calderón's *El mágico prodigioso*.[31] He had a youthful ambition to offer a tragedy to Covent Garden; what became of it remains obscure.[32] In Italy he projected a drama on the life of Tasso, a subject which had also attracted Goethe: 'I have devoted this summer & indeed the next year to the composition of a tragedy on the subject of Tasso's madness, which I find upon inspection is, if properly treated, admirably dramatic & poetical'.[33] Only a few lines survive but the tragedy seems to have been one of the tributaries which flowed into *Julian and Maddalo*. Most of Shelley's plays were not intended for the theatre and none were produced during his lifetime.

Keats's dramatic output was much more slender but both his plays were clearly intended for the theatre. With the help of his friend Charles Brown, to whose plot he was 'Midwife',[34] he completed the historical drama *Otho the Great* (1819), which centred on the Roman emperor who had briefly attracted the interest of Shelley in 1817. The play was sent to Drury Lane where, according to Brown, it was 'accepted, with a promise . . . to bring it forward during that very season' and Edmund Kean 'desired to play the principal character'. In the event, there was a delay and *Otho* was revised and sent to Covent Garden 'whence it was speedily returned with a note, in a boy's hand-writing, containing a negative'.[35] In 1819 Keats also worked on the fragmentary tragedy *King Stephen*. Some years earlier the same subject had interested Coleridge, who planned to make it the basis of an historical drama 'in the manner of Shakespere'.[36] Although Keats did not survive to carry this enterprise to a conclusion, he is not untypical of the Romantic poets in his concern with the historical and particularly with the tragic.

This brief history suggests a number of interesting conclusions. First, the quantity of plays is quite surprising in a generation which had so little direct connection with the theatre. Most of the plays were not intended for performance and all of those which *were* fell short of their intentions, yet the lure of theatrical success is a theme which recurs sufficiently often to deserve some attention. The main attractions were the hope of securing Edmund Kean to play the leading part and the dazzling prospect of financial reward. The variations on these themes are diverse and fascinating. Consider again from a slightly different perspective the examples of Coleridge and of Keats. In January 1813 Coleridge was able to report to his wife on a double success in London. He had concluded a series of lectures 'most triumphantly, with loud, long, & enthusiastic applauses at my Entrance, & ditto in yet fuller Chorus as and for some minutes after I had retired'. Without stopping, the letter goes on to record the applause of another audience:

I suppose, that no dramatic Author ever had so large a number of unsolicited, unknown, yet *predetermined* Plauditors in the Theatre, as I had on Saturday Night. One of the malignant Papers asserted, that I had collected all the *Saints* from Mile End Turnpike to Tyburn Bar. With so many warm Friends it is imposible in the present state of human Nature, that I should not have many unprovoked & unknown Enemies.—You will have heard, that on my entering the Box on Saturday Night I was discovered by the Pit — & that they all turned their faces towards our Box, & gave a treble chear of Claps. I mention these things, because it will please Southey to hear that there is a large number of Persons in London, who hail with enthusiasm any prospect of the Stage's being purified & rendered classical. My success, *if* I succeed (of which, I assure you, I entertain doubts in my opinion well-founded, both from the want of a prominent Actor for Ordonio, & from the want of vulgar Pathos in the Play itself — nay, there is not enough even of *true* dramatic Pathos) but if I succeed, I succeed for others as well as for myself.— [37]

It is almost as if the evening in the lecture room and the evening in the theatre had become one and Coleridge's 'Lecture Box' and his box in the theatre had been fused by the synthetic powers of his imagination into a point of elevation for the receipt of admiration and applause. Here one can find one of the very rare examples of a direct and personal relationship between a Romantic writer and his audience, the heady and dangerous kind of experience which became essential to Dickens in his later years. Clearly, Coleridge was moved and excited by his reception in the theatre but he was also keenly alert to its financial implications, telling Mrs Coleridge that she could have £100 immediately followed by another £100 within a month '& I hope likewise before Midsummer, if God grant me life, to repay you whatever you have expended for the children'. Some independent confirmation is provided by Henry Crabb Robinson, who attended the first performance and the lecture and who records the enthusiasm of the two audiences. Crabb Robinson also records that Coleridge was to receive £100 for the third, sixth, ninth and twentieth nights of the performance; he notes that 'under management he might have obtained another £100 from the theatre'.[38] For an impoverished ' "Author by Trade" ' who was 'forced to write for bread'[39] financial security was necessarily a major consideration yet Coleridge's letter seems to show that he was sensitive to implications that were much less pressingly personal: he hoped that his own success might be a sign that the contemporary stage could still be rescued from the vitiating influences and pressures of a more vulgar kind of popularity.

Unfortunately these high hopes were to remain unrealized. In practice Coleridge seems to have felt encouraged to hope both for popularity and for financial success. His correspondence shows that he was willing to go to considerable lengths to make *Zapolya* into a successful vehicle for the theatre. He told Sotheby: 'It will not be as interesting in the Closet, as the Remorse — I mean, that it is less a Poem — but I hope, it will be proportionally more so on the stage. All passages of independent or ornamental beauty I purposely avoided.'[40] But his ambitions were much more extensive than this and much more surprising since they came from a poet who hoped that the drama might be purified and redeemed. He had a keen sense of what the stage might require and his recurrent interest in such matters was clearly associated with his hopes for 'a smooth & not dishonorable road to competence'. On his voyage to Malta, for example, he jotted down two ideas for the theatre: 'A Tragedy; scene Malta' and, with an eye to entertainment, 'An Afterpiece called or at least the Scene layed at GIBRALTAR — with Scenery, Cavern, &c, would be sure to answer'. Encouraged by the acceptance of *Remorse* he told Crabb Robinson in December 1812: 'It is my hope & purpose to devote a certain portion of my Time for the next twelve months to theatrical attempts, & chiefly in the melodrama, or *comic opera* kind — & from Goethe ... I expect no trifling assistance'.[41] Perhaps his most audacious plans involved the possibility of adapting three plays for the contemporary stage. The first was *Richard II* 'into which I had intended to have introduced a female Character, & to have attempted the giving a *theatrical* Interest to a Play, which for the *closet* is already among the most perfect of Shakespeare's'. Coleridge explained that, although *Richard II* was 'perhaps the most admirable of Shakespear's historical plays', it was also 'the least *representable* in the present state of postulates of the stage'; the main factors were not only 'the entire absence of female Interest' but 'the length of the speeches' and '(with one splendid exception) its want of visual effect'. This general judgement is confirmed in the more disinterested context of his notes on Shakespeare where he concludes that the play is 'ill-suited to our present large theatres' not only because of the length and number of speeches but because 'the events are all *historical*, presented in their *results*, not produced by acts seen, or that take place before the audience'.[42] Yet if the critical judgement remains consistent, there is some irony in the fact that the plans to accommodate the play to the taste of the age were laid by a man who was not grieved at the enormous size and monopoly of the theatres since they 'drove Shakespeare from the stage, to find his proper place in the heart and in the closet'.[43]

The second play was Beaumont and Fletcher's *Pilgrim* which Coleridge planned to rewrite almost entirely, while retaining the outline of the plot and the main characters; the scene was to be placed in Ireland and the play renamed *Love's Metamorphoses*. The third play was Beaumont and Fletcher's *The Beggar's Bush* of which Coleridge entertained 'the greatest hopes'. By 15 October 1815 Coleridge reported that this *rifacimento* was more than half written and that he could complete it in less than a month. He claimed that the first act was entirely his own while in the others at least three-fifths of the language and thought were original. He also noted that 'I had purposely given a prominence to one character (& the want of a *prominent* Character is one grievous Defect both of this & some others of Beaumont & Fletcher's best plays) with a view to Mr Kean'. *The Beggar's Bush* had been selected because he 'was struck with the application of the Fable to the present Times'.[44]

In spite of such signs of energetic optimism, Coleridge was unluckily anticipated by more enterprising rivals and his plans came to nothing. *The Beggar's Bush* was performed at Drury Lane as *The Merchant of Bruges* in December 1815 with Kean in the cast.[45] Kean also appeared in a version of *Richard II* by Richard Wroughton which was first performed on 9 March 1815 and received 13 performances and a review by Hazlitt: 'It is only the *pantomime* part of tragedy ... that which gives the greatest opportunity for "inexpressible dumb-show and noise," which is sure to tell, and tell completely on the stage.' [46] Apparently, Coleridge was undeterred by these misfortunes and he continued to exercise a faculty for the naming and invention of projects which was characteristically fertile. In October 1815 he presented Byron with a curious catalogue of theatrical ideas which he had found among his papers:

1. Two Acts and the Skeleton of the Remainder of a Tragi-comedy, entitled Love and Loyalty.—I wrote it with a view to Stage Effect—& that merit, I think, it would have—

2. Laugh till you lose him—a dramatic Romance—. Putting all merit out of the Question, it is in the scheme more analogous to the Tempest than any other. The Songs, & one act written.
  3. An entertainment in two acts—the Scene in Arabia—First act finished, & the Songs for the second.
  4. The Three Robbers, a Mime or speaking Ballet—for Christmas.
  5. A scheme at large for a Pantomime—from a Story in the Tartarian Tales, which delighted me when a Boy.—[47]

This list is intriguing since some of the items at least can be traced back to a much earlier stage of Coleridge's career. The first item is probably to be equated with *The Triumph of Loyalty* which was closely based on a play by the Spanish dramatist Antonio Coëllo; a prose summary appears in one of the notebooks while a draft of nearly 400 lines survives in manuscript. Coleridge amused, or tantalized, himself with thoughts of a great theatrical triumph: he drew up an imposing title-page on which he noted that the play was 'first performed with universal applause at the Theatre Royal, Drury Lane, on Saturday, February the 7th, 1801'. A very distinguished cast-list which included Mrs Siddons and the Kembles was appended. In 1817 he was to resurrect the play by printing 'A Night Scene. A Dramatic Fragment' in *Sibylline Leaves*, where it was dated 1813. This dating might perhaps suggest that he had tried to revise the play during the period of his success with *Remorse*.[48] *Laugh Till You Lose Him* was in his thoughts in October 1805 but is otherwise obscure.[49] The 'entertainment' with 'the Scene in Arabia' is elsewhere referred to as *Diadestè the Arabia Rite* and can be traced back at least as far as December 1803; a sketch and a heavily corrected draft of a scene or two still survive. Both can be dated after 1812.[50] The 'speaking Ballet' appears to be a proposition which is wonderfully Coleridgean; but Hazlitt reviewed a Drury Lane production called *Shakspear versus Harlequin* which was billed as 'a speaking pantomime' so it is possible that Coleridge was exploiting a recognized theatrical mode. In any event he was alert to the generic paradox, and in another letter he acknowledged that 'I cannot call it a Pantomime but a Hemimime — a sort of splendid speaking Pantomime'.[51] But here as so often with Coleridge, a shadow seems to have fallen between the idea and the execution. The whole case presents no adjunct to the Muses' diadem but it is highly instructive because it reveals so clearly the influence which might be exerted by the conditions of the nineteenth-century stage and by its requirements for popular success.

The case of Keats is very different but his ambitions also included an element of the economic: 'Mine I am sure is a tolerable tragedy — it would have been a bank to me, if just as I had finish'd it I had not heard of Kean's resolution to go to America. . . . There is no actor can do the principal character besides Kean.' The conjunction is sufficiently familiar and unsurprising. As always with Keats, however, there is the inescapable question of fame: 'Were it to succeed . . . it would lift me out of the mire. I mean the mire of a bad reputation'.[52] Gradually, Keats's intuitive and brilliantly particularized reading of Shakespeare seems to have convinced him that only as a dramatist could he aspire towards the pinnacle of poetic achievement but he felt only too oppressively the insufficiency of his own 'little dramatic skill'. Writing in November 1819 he admitted that his dramatic talents were as yet undeveloped though they might be 'sufficient for a Poem'; he could prepare himself for the Shakespearean challenge by diffusing 'the colouring of St Agnes eve throughout a Poem in which Character and Sentiment would be the figures to such drapery'. The poetry was conceived as a series of stepping-stones towards a higher ambition: 'Two or three such Poems . . . written in the course of the next six years would be a famous gradus ad Parnassum altissimum . . . they would nerve me up to the writing of a few fine Plays — my greatest ambition — when I do feel ambitious.'[53]

In the pursuit of this goal Keats was almost certainly influenced by his very brief but intense experience as the theatrical critic of *The Champion*. Like so many of his contemporaries, he was delighted and inspired by the acting of Kean:

A melodious passage in poetry is full of pleasures both sensual and spiritual. . . . The sensual life of verse springs warm from the lips of Kean, and to one learned in Shakespearian hieroglyphics, — learned in the spiritual portion of those lines to which Kean adds a sensual grandeur; his tongue must seem to have robbed 'the Hybla bees, and left them honeyless.'[54]

This comes close to Byron's response to Kean's performance as Iago: 'I am acquainted with no *im*material sensuality so delightful as good acting'.[55] But 'the sensual life of verse' reveals an interest in the life of language which is characteristically Keatsian, as is his emphasis on 'the indescribable gusto in his voice', and on the dissolving of the boundaries of self under the influence of great emotion: 'Kean delivers himself up to the instant feeling, without a shadow of a thought about any thing else.'[56] It has been plausibly argued that the experience of Kean's acting helped Keats to formulate the concept of Negative Capability, a quality 'which Shakespeare posessed so enormously'.[57] The example of Kean also generated heroic longings in the poet, not simply to make him the inspiration and central focus of a dramatic world, but to achieve a literary distinction which was analogous to the actor's and which would signal the beginning of a new literary epoch as decisively as the appearance of Kean had marked the end of 'the Kemble religion' and the initiation of a style which was imaginatively new and compelling: 'One of my Ambitions is to make as great a revolution in modern dramatic writing as Kean has done in acting'.[58] Such ambitions led, inevitably perhaps, to thoughts of Shakespeare and the poetic drama.

As the poets were only too well aware, there had been little or no significant verse drama in England since the seventeenth century; the awakening of new poetic energies propelled them not only to develop and extend the established forms of poetry but to explore the possibilities of creating a drama which could draw its strength from what Shelley described as the 'peculiar style of intense and comprehensive imagery which distinguishes the modern literature of England'.[59] Such an aim involved not only the question of contemporary relevance but the felt necessity to reconnect with the tradition of Shakespeare and his contemporaries, to demonstrate the centrality and the significance of the new literature by challenging the great achievements of the past. Shelley put it forcefully in the *Defence of Poetry*:

The drama being that form under which a greater number of modes of expression of poetry are susceptible of being combined than any other, the connexion of poetry and social good is more observable in the drama than in whatever other form: and it is indisputable that the highest perfection of human society has ever corresponded with the highest dramatic excellence; and that the corruption or the extinction of the drama in a nation where it has once flourished, is a mark of a corruption of manners, and an extinction of the energies which sustain the soul of social life. But, as Machiavelli says of political insitutions, that life may be preserved and renewed, if men should arise capable of bringing back the drama to its principles. And this is true with respect to poetry in its most extended sense: all language, institution and form, require not only to be produced but to be sustained: the office and character of a poet participates in the divine nature as regards providence, no less than as regards creation.[60]

This, of course, represents an ideal — and one senses here and elsewhere in the *Defence* that it is an ideal towards which Shelley aspires with an all-too-wistful sense of the limitations of his own age — but it is important because it unflinchingly articulates a case for the social and political relevance of the poetic drama. If such a drama were to 'sustain the soul of social life', it would not take the form, one assumes, of a drama exclusively intended for the printed page or the closet but it would be an influential part of public life, a creativity in which everyone could share.

Sometimes aspirations such as these involved the model of the Greek drama whose virtues and their intimate connection with the wholeness and health of Athenian society were eloquently and influentially formulated by A. W. Schlegel in his *Lectures on Dramatic Literature*, which appeared in English translation in 1815.[61] Inescapably, it involved the example of Shakespeare whose potency as a direct influence had been largely avoided in the eighteenth century and whose plays were still regularly performed in versions which were truncated, reshaped and often heavily revised and rewritten. Radical 'translations' such as Nahum Tate's version of *King Lear* continued to hold the stage. Tate's version, which was first published in 1681, omitted the Fool and inserted a happy ending; rival versions by Garrick and Colman did little to shake its popularity and, except for relatively slight variations, it was the received version in the theatre until Macready reverted to the Shakespearean text in 1834 (but without the Fool). Nor was this exceptional. Even so scholarly an actor as John Philip Kemble performed *Richard III* in the version by Colley Cibber in which Shakespeare's text was cut, rearranged, significantly reinterpreted, and embellished by seven soliloquies of Cibber's invention. By a significant irony, the new energy and urgency of Romantic poetry was due, in part, to an ability to rediscover the Shakespearean possibilities of the language, which had been inhibited and checked by the canons of eighteenth century taste, and repressed and flattened by the adaptors and the translators. It was essential to widen the range of linguistic possibility and to escape from those narrow criteria of propriety which had caused even so acute a critic as Dr Johnson to object to Macbeth's knife as 'an instrument used by butchers and cooks in the meanest employments' and to censure 'the blanket of the dark' as risibly inappropriate to the tragic context.[62] Coleridge exclaimed in one of his notebooks: 'One would suppose from Johnson's Preface that Sh. was a pie-bald Poet — & that he, the Critic, was standing by, in the worthy employment of counting & pointing out, black spot against white . . . — O the spirit of envy & baseness & more than all, indolence of heart & mind amounting to & manifesting itself in an impotence of *intelligent* admiration . . . & . . . in pointing out as faults the conditio sine quâ non of the acknowleged beauties! — The expecting of contradictions!'

Yet the liberation of poetic language did not always coincide with the liberation of the drama; the Shakespearean model was fatal for most of the lesser dramatists of the period, who were classified by Coleridge as 'the tragic Dwarfs, which exhausted Nature seems to have been under the necessity of producing since Shakespear'.[64] The Shakespearean ambition sometimes inflicted serious damage not only on dwarfs but on their more gifted contemporaries. The long list of verse dramatists includes Henry Hart Milman whose *Fazio* was printed in 1815, performed first at the Surrey Theatre in 1816-17 as *The Italian Wife* and ultimately under its original title at Covent Garden in 1818. Shelley greatly admired the performance of Eliza O'Neill in the role of the heroine; Thomas Love Peacock remembered his 'absorbed attention' to the actress who, as Mary Shelley claimed, was 'always in his thoughts' when he was creating the character of Beatrice in *The Cenci*. Peacock also observed that 'With the exception of *Fazio*, I do not remember his having been pleased with any performance at an English theatre'.[65] Another successful verse dramatist was the Irish novelist Charles Robert Maturin, author of *Melmoth the Wanderer*, whose *Bertram* was performed at Drury Lane in 1816 with Kean in the title role and which achieved great success both on the stage and in printed form where it went through seven editions in a year. Maturin's play had the effect of focusing the critical faculties and the creative energies of more gifted contemporaries who recognized its inferiority. Shelley was sure that his own play on Tasso would have 'better morality than Fazio, & better poetry than Bertram, at least' and one of his objections to the calumniating critics in the Preface to *Adonais* was that they 'in their venal good nature, presumed to draw a parallel between the Rev. Mr. Milman and Lord Byron'.[66] Coleridge was offended because Drury Lane had lavished its attention on *Bertram* while failing to accept *Zapolya* which Byron had encouraged him to submit: 'Perhaps, I might be supposed to feel this the more from the extreme splendor, with which that infamous Abortion of Ignorance and Jacobinism, the Bertram, was *got up* — a rank vapor from the condemned Hole of the pseudo-poetic Newgate, on which all the colors of the Rain-bow were made to play, and one scene (that of the storm) introduced merely as a Picture'.[67] He also recorded a piece of offensively backhanded encouragement which exposed the aesthetic limitations and the insincerity which prevailed in the theatrical world: ' "No expence can be too great (so I was informed by one of the Restorers of the *classical* character of old Drury) for it is nearly equal to Shakespear, & it's success will be a fine thing for *you*, Sir! since tho' *such* a Tragedy may not perhaps be presented, yet it will open out the way to the Shakespearian Style." '[68] Coleridge was so deeply provoked that he submitted a long analysis of the deficiencies of Maturin's play to *The Courier*; the piece was later reprinted in Chapter 23 of *Biographia Literaria* although, through a curious, if characteristic, reluctance to take full responsibility, Coleridge continued to disclaim it as his own.

Whatever the shortcomings of *Bertram* or *Fazio*, the lure of the verse drama exercised a great fascination on the major writers of the period, particularly on those who belonged to the second generation. This concentration on the poetic and the ambition to carry on the traditions of Shakespeare or the Greeks coincided with a number of other factors to prevent any significant attempt to develop or to revive the traditions of comedy. The poet best qualified to succeed in the comic mode was Byron, who might have been expected to add something to the comedy of manners which had received such a brief but potent injection of life from his friend Sheridan in the 1770s. Byron's letters and journals show that he had a sharp eye for the comic absurdities of human behaviour and the hypocrisies and inert conventions of society. He also possessed a highly-developed faculty for dramatizing both his own role and the kaleidoscopic scenes of high and low life which he recorded for his correspondents. His ear was as sharp as his eye and he alone of the Romantic poets could have realized Yeats's desire for 'the greatest possible knowledge of the speech . . . of the world'. Yet Byron's own ambitions for theatrical success appear to have been directed to higher things. He translated one scene from Goldoni and drafted a few scenes for a comedy of his own but both of these projects were abandoned. Perhaps he was responding to the shift in taste which had caused Sheridan himself to retire from comedy when he entered politics (his only susequent play was *Pizarro*, a spectacular adaptation of Kotzebue which was performed with great success in 1799, although Coleridge labelled it 'a Pantomime' [69]). Perhaps he was responding to what some observers interpreted as degeneration of comedy into farce and of comic actors into buffoons. This downward trend was chronicled by Leigh Hunt: 'The scene is so far drawn forward, as it were, into the part appropriated to the audience, or, in other words, it is so evidently the intention of the author, and consequently of his actors, to stand before the spectator as mere candidates for applause, that the stage becomes literally abstracted from its abstraction.' Comedy had lost its traditional moral function and had been transformed from a polished mirror into 'a glass full of excrescences and undulations, in which the human figure becomes a mere laughable monstrosity'.[70] The general consensus was that these alterations in the emphasis and tone of comedy had been produced by changes in the structure of society, which in turn affected the conditions of theatrical success. 'The new comedy, increasingly bourgeois in its attitudes and characters, had no significant place for the fine gentleman of a previous age; it was anything but genteel. Neither was the acting, nor could it be. Bustling, extravagant, noisy, emotional, and cut of a coarser cloth than its predecessor, this comedy found superb actors who could perfectly express its style and content.' [71]

The characteristics of this new style of acting are precisely and tellingly recorded by Leigh Hunt in 'An Essay on the Appearance, Causes and Consequences of the Decline of British Comedy', in *Critical Essays on the Performers of the London Theatre* (1807), in a general survey in *The Reflector* (1811) and in a long series of review in *The Examiner*. The coarsening and exaggeration of style seems to have been influenced by the size of the theatres and by the desire to produce an effect; the consequences could be observed not only in performances of the lesser dramatists, whose very deficiencies may have helped to create the style, but also in the plays of their superiors:

> If the principal characters of REYNOLDS and of DIBDIN are always out of nature, their representation... must be unnatural also; and as our comic actors are perpetually employed upon these punchinellos, as they are always labouring to grimace and grin them into applause, they become habituated and even partial to their antics, and can never afterwards separate the effect from the means, the applause from the unnatural style of acting. The extravagance therefore of look and gesture, so necessary to the caricatures of our farci-comic writers, they cannot help carrying into the characters of our best dramatists, to which it is every way injurious.[72]

It may have been this 'extravagance... of look and gesture' which Coleridge had in mind when he wrote a letter of congratulation and advice to the actor Charles Mathews, a celebrated comic performer who was best known for his chameleonic gifts for impersonation. Coleridge praises the performance of Mathews in the role of Sir Archy MacSarcasm but notes that it is a duplicate of an earlier performance by Cooke: it is, says Coleridge,

> so very excellent, that if I were intimate with you, I should get angry and abuse you for not forming for yourself some *original* & important character—The man, who could so impersonate Sir Archy McSarcasm might do *any thing* in *profound* Comedy (i.e. that which gives us the *passions* of men & their endless modifications & influences on Thoughts, Gestures, &c, modified in their turn by Circumstances of Rank, Relations, Nationality &c, instead of mere transitory manners—in short, the inmost man represented on the superficies, instead of the Superficies merely representing itself.)—[73]

In the same year Coleridge laments the failure of the playwright George Colman the Younger who 'possessed the elements of dramatic power in a far higher degree, than Sheridan': 'The play is assuredly the very sediment, the dregs, of a noble Cask of Wine: for such *was* ? yes, in *many* instances *was* & has been; and in many more *might* have been, COLMAN'S Dramatic Genius'.[74] Both the mourning over Colman's wasted talents and the advice to Mathews suggest that Coleridge was sharply aware of the limitations and weakness of contemporary comedy yet his reference to '*profound* Comedy' indicates that he was opposed not to the comic in general, but to the conditions and influences which prevailed in the theatre. Comedy, it seemed, might still be redeemed and purified.

Such a transformation never occurred, with the result that the comic gifts of writers such as Byron and Peacock were lost to the stage. The forces which helped to cause so notable a lacuna in dramatic ambition probably reached beyond Shakespearean ambitions and the discouraging coarsening of taste and performance to a deeper uncertainty, an antipathy to the comic mode itself which can be detected in a number of the major poets. Peacock's *Memoirs of Percy Bysshe Shelley* anatomize a classic instance. Peacock records that Shelley possessed a sense of humour but only exercised it within limits which were strictly defined:

> Shelley, when he did laugh, laughed heartily, the more so as what he considered the perversions of comedy excited not his laughter but his indignation, although such disgusting outrages on taste and feeling as the burlesques by which the stage is now disgraced had not then been perpetrated. The ludicrous, when it neither offended good feeling, nor perverted moral judgment, necessarily presented itself to him with greater force.[75]

The problem was complicated by the fact that Shelley 'had a prejudice against theatres' which Peacock struggled to overcome. When he induced Shelley to attend a performance of *The School for Scandal* Shelley could not suspend his natural impatience beyond the fourth act: ' "I see the purpose of this comedy. It is to associate virtue with bottles and glasses, and villainy with books." [76] I had great difficulty to make him stay to the end. He often talked of "the withering and perverting spirit of comedy" '. The antipathy seems to have extended beyond the theatre to the very spirit of comedy itself. Peacock notes that he 'tried in vain to reconcile him to comedy'. When he quoted Michael Perez's soliloquy from Beaumont and Fletcher's *Rule a Wife and Have a Wife*, Shelley responded:

> 'There is comedy in its perfection. Society grinds down poor wretches into the dust of abject poverty, till they are scarcely recognizable as human beings; and then, instead of being treated as what they really are, subjects of the deepest pity, they are brought forward as grotesque monstrosities to be laughed at.' I said, 'You must admit the fineness of

the expression.' 'It is true,' he answered; 'but the finer it is the worse it is, with such a perversion of sentiment.' [77]

The moral disapproval was consistent and caused Shelley to reject the comedy of the Restoration, one of the period in which 'the calculating principle pervades all forms of dramatic exhibition':

Comedy loses its ideal universality: wit succeeds to humour; we laugh from self-complacency and triumph instead of pleasure; malignity, sarcasm and contempt, succeed to sympathetic merriment; we hardly laugh, but we smile. Obscenity, which is ever blasphemy against the divine beauty in life, becomes, from the very veil which it assumes, more active if less disgusting: it is a monster for which the corruption of society for ever brings forth new food, which it devours in secret.[78]

In this case Shelley's critique still carries a recognizable flavour of puritanical superiority; but it is more radical and more firmly based on an understanding of the social forces which helped to produce the prevailing codes of wit.

Shelley may appear to be an extreme case but his political and moral reservations were shared to a greater or lesser degree by a number of his contemporaries. The Romantics were too strongly opposed to the prevailing systems or too intimately involved in a struggle to defend what they considered its better elements to be amused or entertained by the way of the world. An age of war and revolution did not allow them the detachment necessary to observe the spectacle from an ironic distance. For Shelley, at least, to allow himself to be amused was in some way to collaborate with or acquiesce in the perpetuation of an unjust social order of which he profoundly disapproved. In the *Defence of Poetry* he offered a concession to the comic where it was envisaged not as a genre in its own right but as an element in a greater whole: 'The modern practice of blending comedy with tragedy, though liable to great abuse in point of practise, is undoubtedly an extension of the dramatic circle; but the comedy should be as in King Lear, universal, ideal, and sublime'.[79] This formulation is far removed from 'the daily intercourse of all this unintelligible world' (to adopt Hazlitt's version of Wordsworth); it deliberately avoids or transcends Coleridge's 'mere transitory manners' or 'the Superficies merely representing itself'. Some sense of what Shelley may have had in mind can be deduced from *Charles the First* where Shelley attempts his own blend of the comic and the tragic and where the character of Archy the jester owes an obvious debt to Shakespeare's Fool. In itself this constitutes a break with contemporary taste since the Fool was not restored to a staged performance of *Lear* till 1838, when the part was played by an actress.

Such tendencies cannot be explained in any simple fashion or attributed to any single factor. They were the product of a variety of forces and influences, cultural, psychological, literary and political; as Shelley put it, 'Poets . . . are in one sense the creators and in another the creations of their age.' [80] It would be foolish, therefore, to insist on an explanation which was merely mechanical; but it would also be wrong to neglect the influence of the conditions which prevailed in the contemporary theatre. These, too, were subject to the spirit of change. The old structures and relationships which had characterized the eighteenth-century theatre were shifting and forming themselves into new patterns. In the eighteenth century the audience could have been charted roughly according to class:

> In 1750 and for many years thereafter, the class divisions among audiences were directly related to the seats they occupied in the auditorium, as had been the case a long time before 1750. The upper classes still sat in the front and side boxes; the 'critics' and professional men, civil servants, tradesmen and a general cross-section of the middle class in the pit and lower gallery; the working class, including servants, journeymen, apprentices, sailors and their women-folk, in the upper gallery.[81]

These divisions were subject to some variation but in general the social stratification of the theatre audience seemed to provide a tangible demonstration of the principle of decorum which still exercised so much influence over literary production. This distinctly articulated but organic unity gradually began to change so that the audience which the Romantics knew and towards which they addressed themselves had suffered a sharp and significant dislocation. Towards the end of the eighteenth century 'the predominant pattern of taste was that of an educated middle-class audience leavened with aristocratic spice, and the repertory on the whole was constructed accordingly'. Writing in 1850, Leigh Hunt remembered the period of his youth when 'People of all times of life were much greater playgoers than they are now':

They dined earlier, they had not so many newspapers, clubs, and pianofortes; the French Revolution only tended at first to endear the nation to its own habits; it had not yet opened a thousand new channels of thought and interest; nor had railroads conspired to carry people, bodily as well as mentally, into as many analogous directions. Everything was more concentrated, and the various classes of society felt a greater concern in the same amusements. Nobility, gentry, citizens, princes, — all were frequenters of theatres, and even more or less acquainted personally with the performers. Nobility intermarried with them; gentry, and citizens too, wrote for them; princes conversed and lived with them.[82]

Some time after the beginning of the nineteenth century the upper-class influence began to fade and the opera became more fashionable than the legitimate drama. While this had the effect of making the theatres more truly popular in some senses, it also tended towards a broadening and coarsening of effects; contemporary observers noted with regret that the old balance of forces within the audience could no longer serve as a corrective and a generously distributed criterion of taste. Writing in 1811 Leigh Hunt suggested that the 'degeneracy of the drama' could partly be attributed to changes in the nation itself. He wondered whether 'the general diffusion of letters [i.e. literacy]' had not contributed to the decline.

The English public, never much attached to theatrical amusements, and at best inclined to consider them as objects of mere relaxation, seemed to have been more than ever diverted from any care on the subject by the encreasing interest of politics. Commerce too, as it advanced, by no means tended to enlarge their ideas on any subject; and it is curious to observe, how our comedies of late, sentimental as well as farcical, have run upon the manners and moral feelings of shopkeepers. With the gentlemen of small independent fortunes, vanished a great deal of taste as well as of public spirit . . .[83]

Such a lament for ancient certainties cannot be entirely exempted from the charge of elitism or of nostalgia for a pre-revolutionary world where aristocratic values predominated. Yet the decline was undeniable; and it was clearly expressed in and accelerated by the new relation between the audience and the stage. The old intimacy of relationship between the actors and the audience was lost. As Hunt recognized, this also involved the gradual migration of the critics from the pit to the boxes, where 'it is not reckoned very decorous to express any vehement opinion of what is going forward on the stage'.[84]

The pattern of redistribution can be clearly traced in contemporary illustrations. Rowlandson's aquatint of Covent Garden in 1786 may provide a characteristically heightened sense of the energy of the audience and of the varieties of its local life but it also conveys a vivid sense of the vitality of the theatre as a place of entertainment and of its capacity to allow for a sense of intimacy and involvement. The audience seems to be very much part of the action (which might remind us how for social observers and caricaturists such as Rowlandson and Hogarth the performance of the audience was in itself a rich contribution to the 'theatre' of contemporary life).[85] A picture of Holland's Covent Garden in 1804 provides a clear indication of how things had changed.[86] Even if we allow for the exaggerated dynamism of Rowlandson's line in the earlier picture, the later scene presents an audience which is obviously more detached from the action on the stage: in particular, there is now a gap between the stage and the pit and the intimate relationship between the actors and the pit appears to have been lost. The main reason for such changes was the increased size of the theatre. Between 1792 and 1812 Covent Garden and Drury Lane, which were the two centres of 'legitimate' drama in London, were both burnt down and went through a process of alteration and rebuilding with consequences which were deplored by many men of letters and sympathetic observers of the drama. When Covent Garden was rebuilt after a fire in 1808 it had a pit and five galleries and could seat 2,800. When the third Drury Lane opened in 1794 it could seat 3,611; in its fourth manifestation which opened in 1812 its capacity had been reduced to 2,283.[87] The essential case against the size of these theatres was forcefully expressed by Walter Scott in an 'Essay on the Drama' (1819) in which he explains the factors which depress the national drama at a point when 'the age has no reason to apprehend any decay of dramatic talent':

The *first* inconvenience arises from the great size of the theatres, which has rendered them unfit for the legitimate purposes of the Drama. The persons of the performers are, in these huge circles, so much diminished, that nothing short of the mask and buskin could render them distinctly visible to the audience. Show and machinery have therefore usurped the place of tragic poetry; and the author is compelled to address himself to the eyes, not to the understanding or feelings of the spectators. This is of itself a gross error. Everything beyond correct costume and theatrical decorum is foreign to the legitimate purposes of the Drama, as tending to divide the attention of the audience; and the rivalry of the scene-painter and the carpenter cannot be very flattering to any author or actor of genius. Besides, all attempts at decoration, beyond what the decorum of the piece requires, must end in paltry puppet-show exhibition. The talents of the scene-painter and the mechanist cannot, owing to the very nature of the stage, make battles, sieges, &c., anything but objects of ridicule. Thus we have enlarged our theatres, so as to destroy the effect of acting, without carrying to any perfection that of pantomime and dumb show.[88]

The Romantic theatre was remarkable for the talents of its scene designers and for the inventive skills of its engineers; yet, as Scott rightly recognized, the combined effect was to divert the attention from the intellectual to the sensational and from the subtle to the immediately apprehensible.[89] The highest values were provided by the merely external and the superficial. Everything aspired to the condition of spectacle with the result that 'The author is compelled to address himself to the eyes, not to the understanding or feelings of the spectators'. Scott's criticism not only finds fault with the means but it also seems to reveal a symptomatic unease with the nature of the theatrical; an austere recoiling from the essentially illusory nature of the stage, which can be found even in writers such as Lamb and Hazlitt, who rejoiced in the drama and in theatrical performance. Compare, for example, Hazlitt's response to a performance of *A Midsummer Night's Dream*: 'All that is fine in the play, was lost in the representation. The spirit was evaporated, the genius was fled; but the spectacle was fine . . . Oh, ye scene-shifters, ye scene-painters, ye machinists and dress-makers, ye manufacturers of moon and stars that give no light, ye musical composers, ye men in the orchestra, fiddlers and trumpeters and players on the double drum and loud bassoon, rejoice!' [90] Or Lamb's impatience with the staging of *The Tempest*: 'Spirits and fairies cannot be represented, they cannot even be painted, — they can only be believed. But the elaborate and anxious provision of scenery, which the luxury of the age demands, in these cases works a quite contrary effect to what is intended. That which in comedy, or plays of familiar life, adds so much to the life of the imitation, in plays which appeal to the higher faculties, positively destroys the illusion which it is introduced to aid.' [92] Or his irritation at the intrusive inadequacy of costumes in *Macbeth*: 'I remember the last time I saw Macbeth played, the discrepancy I felt at the changes of garment which he varied, — the shiftings and re-shiftings, like a Romish priest at mass. The luxury of stage-improvements, and the importunity of the public eye, require this'.[93] Criticisms such as these seem to be rooted in a suspicion that there is a fundamental incompatibility between the demands of public performance and the aspirations of literature. As Hazlitt put it: 'Poetry and the stage do not agree together'.[94] This gap was essentially unbridgeable but it was exaggerated and widened by the tendencies of theatrical production.

Not only did this involve a seeking after effects which could never be more than crudely and mechanically mimetic but it also displaced and devalued the word. This concern was shared by Coleridge who declared in one of his lectures that he 'never saw any of Shakespeare's plays performed, but with a degree of pain, disgust, and indignation' and who underlined the incompatibility between Shakespeare's plays and the prevailing conditions of the stage where a scene could be 'introduced merely as a picture'. In Shakespeare the 'length of the speeches was adapted to a delivery between acting and recitation, which produced in the auditors a docility or frame of mind favorable to the poet, and useful to themselves'; in contrast, modern productions were designed to prevent the audience from concentrating since in 'the glare of the scenes, with every wished-for object industriously realized, the mind becomes bewildered in surrounding attractions'.[95] This tyranny of the eye recorded by Scott and Coleridge might also perhaps be connected with the proliferation of Shakespearean illustrations, the most notable example of which was the series of 170 pictures commissioned for the Boydell Shakespeare Gallery, which was initiated in 1786 and published in the form of engravings in 1802.[96] Although the best of these illustrations provided visual interpretations or translations which were imaginatively inventive in their own right, the overall effect was to shift attention from the word to the picture. Lamb thought the illustrations too distractingly vital and preferred the freedom of his own imaginings:

What injury (short of the Theatres) did not Boydell's Shakspeare Gallery do me with Shakspeare? to have Opie's Shakspeare, Northcote's Shakspeare, light-headed Fuselis' Shakspeare, heavy-headed Romney's Shakspeare, wooden-headed West's Shakspeare (tho' he did the best in

Lear) deaf-headed Reynolds's Shakspeare, instead of my, and every body's Shakspeare, To be tied down to an authentic face of Juliet! To have Imogen's portrait! to confine the illimitable!⁹⁷

Lamb objected to the picture usurping the words; although he would not have complained, they also usurped the prerogative of the stage since they were, for the most part, idealized and abstracted from the reality of performance. The plays were therefore confirmed as books, as words on a page, rather than as scripts for actors.

The great size of the theatres also encouraged a style of acting which tended towards exaggeration and the grand effect. Undoubtedly this was influenced by the problems of projecting the voice to so large an audience but it also accorded with the growing propensity towards the overstated and the melodramatic. John Philip Kemble, Sarah Siddons and Edmund Kean all exercised a powerful hold on the public imagination and embodied the ideals of tragic acting. Kean, in particular, seems to have been acknowledged by his contemporaries both as a performer who was highly skilled in the pointing of his craft and as a force of nature, a creator, a poet in his own right. Watching Kean, said Coleridge, was like reading Shakespeare by flashes of lightning. When he played Sir Giles Overreach he frightened the other actors by the intensity of his performance and caused Byron to have a convulsive fit. Hazlitt, who chronicled his performances in detail, identified the force of his impact as 'some collected and overpowering display of energy or pathos, which electrified at the moment, and left a lasting impression on the mind afterwards'.[98] Kean's capacity for pointing his performance and for achieving the memorable posture reminded Hazlitt of the Boydell Gallery; his performance as Richard the Third in itself presented 'a perpetual succession of striking pictures'.[99] It is not surprising that, as we have seen, the Romantic poets sometimes wrote or planned their plays with Kean in mind; certainly, their notions of performance must have been influenced by his style of acting.

Yet this, too, in its way was an influence which it might have been better to avoid. The dominance of actors like Kean, Mrs Siddons and Kemble represented another form of tyranny over the text; at this period it was still common for the author's name to be omitted from the playbills. In different ways, several of the

Romantics gave voice to their anxiety about the perils of such a star-system and such an insistence on the unique personality of the actor. Coleridge told his lecture audience that the public 'went to see Mr. Kemble in *Macbeth*, or Mrs. Siddons' Isabel, to hear speeches usurped by fellows who owed their very elevation to dexterity in snuffing candles'. His own experience of Siddons and Kemble in *Macbeth* suggested a fundamental rift between Shakespeare and the actors of the contemporary stage: 'these might be the Macbeths of the Kembles, but they were not the Macbeths of Shakespeare'.[100] It was this kind of disappointment which led him to claim that Shakespeare's proper place was not on the stage but in the heart and in the closet. Lamb also took issue with the celebrated performance of Mrs Siddons as Lady Macbeth: 'Mrs. S. never got more fame by any thing than by the manner in which she dismisses the guests in the banquet-scene in Macbeth: it is as much remembered as any of her thrilling tones or impressive looks. But does such a trifle as this enter into the imagination of the readers of that wild and wonderful scene?' Acting and the pressure which it exerts on the spectator to interpret it critically has the effect that all the 'non-essentials are raised into an importance, injurious to the main interest of the play'. Lamb even suggested that 'the sort of pleasure which Shakspeare's plays give in the acting seems to me not at all to differ from that which the audience receive from those of other writers'. 'Is not the female performer as great (as they call it)' in plays by obscure and lesser dramatists as in the works of Shakespeare? [101]

The combined effect of all these factors was to emphasize the visual and the spectacular. At its most elevated, this included the acting of Kean and Mrs Siddons; at its most debased, it involved a crude exploitation of the craving for the melodramatic and the merely sensational. One of the most widely publicized examples was the introduction of horses into the melodrama *Blue Beard* by George Colman the Younger when it was revived at Covent Garden in March 1811. The effect was graphically recorded by Leigh Hunt, who reviewed the performance in *The Examiner* where he offered an analysis of the connection between such spetacles and the size of theatres together with an insight into the underlying economic imperatives:

The success of such exhibitions is not only allowed to be a mark of corrupted taste with regard to better things, but it materially helps to produce that corruption. They are too powerful a stimulus to the senses of the common order of spectators, and take away from their eyes and ears all relish for more delicate entertainment. The managers and the public thus corrupt each other; but it is the former who begin the infection by building these enormous theatres in which a great part of the spectators must have noise and shew before they can hear or see what is going forwards. In time these spectators learn to like nothing else; and then the managers must administer to their depraved appetite, or they cannot get rich. Are these the persons to cry out against the erection of a new and smaller theatre? [102]

Where Shelley's *Defence of Poetry* attributes the decline of comedy to 'the corruption of society', Hunt here places the emphasis on the managers who helped to create a 'depraved taste' in their audiences which in its turn exercises a further corrupting influence on the managers. In the case of Covent Garden the offence was all the greater because the manager was the great John Philip Kemble, 'the *gravis Esopus* of our Stage' as Hunt put it, who 'must turn beasts into actors'. Returning to the subject in July in a review of *Quadrupeds*, Hunt declared that Covent Garden was 'over grown' 'because it is fully ascertained that such large theatres are not fit for a delicate and just representation of the drama, and that they inevitably lead to the substitution of shew for sense'.[103] The condemnation of critics like Hunt was clearly justified but the cycle of cause and effect which he had identified continued to operate with a predictability which seemed almost inevitable. For the Christmas pantomime in that year the unrepentant management introduced an elephant which, according to a contemporary account, was 'highly applauded'.[104]

It was this kind of craving for the spectacular towards which Byron directed his scorn when he composed an 'Address' which was delivered by the actor Robert Elliston at Drury Lane on 10 October 1812. Byron had been invited to provide a suitable piece of verse to celebrate the opening of the theatre which had been destroyed by fire in 1809. He used the occasion not only to mark the rising of a theatrical phoenix and to dwell on the great achievements of the past but also to invite the audience to collaborate in the rehabilitation of dramatic taste and to exercise a judgement which was truly critical and discerning:

> But know—our triumph this alone secures
> The judging voice and eye must first be yours
> Ours to obey your will or right or wrong
> To soar in Sentiment, or creep in song
> Nay lower still—the Drama yet deplores
> That late she deigned to crawl upon 'all fours'
> When Richard roars in Bosworth for a horse
> If you command—the *Steed* must come in course

In the event the management ensured that these lines were omitted from the final version which offered an account of the decadence of early nineteenth-century taste which was not so specific or so pointed in its contempt for the ingloriously fallen state of contemporary drama. The censored version also omitted Byron's rather crudely expressed plea to the audience: 'That public praise be never more disgraced / From babes and brutes redeem a Nation's taste'. Byron's approach represents an interesting variation on the analysis of Leigh Hunt since it emphasizes Byron's belief that the ultimate responsibility for the health of the sinking stage is vested not in the actor, the playwright or the management but in the audience:

> Friends of the stage—to whom both Players and Plays
> Must sue alike for pardon, or for praise—
> Whose judging voice and eye alone direct
> The boundless power to cherish or reject;
> If e'er frivolity had led to fame,
> And made us blush that you forbore to blame—
> If e'er the sinking stage could condescend
> To soothe the sickly taste, it dare not mend—
> All past reproach may present scenes refute,
> And censure, wisely loud, be justly mute!—
> Oh! since your fiat stamps the Drama's laws,
> Forbear to mock us with misplac'd applause;
> So pride shall doubly nerve the actor's powers,
> And reason's voice be echo'd back by ours!—[105]

Reactions such as these can help us to understand both the curiously ambivalent way in which the Romantic poets engaged with the theatre and their comparative inability to create a body of drama which might be able to hold the stage. Three years after writing the 'Address' Byron was invited to join the committee of management at Drury Lane. No other Romantic poet was so close to 'theatre business, management of men' yet his feelings about the compromises of theatrical management and his strong sense of the ludicrous ensured that though his position was entertaining it was always less than comfortable. He recalled this period in his 'Detached Thoughts': 'Then the Scenes I had to go through! — the authours — and the authoresses — — the Milliners — the wild Irishmen — the people from Brighton — from Blackwell — from Chatham — from Cheltenham — from Dublin — from Dundee — who came in upon me! — to all of whom it was proper to give a civil answer — and a hearing — and a reading'. Among the projects there was 'an Irish tragedy in which the unities could not fail to be observed for the protagonist was chained by the leg to a pillar during the chief part of the performance'.[106] In a letter of 1815 he records a night at Drury Lane when he saw *Ina* by Mrs Wilmot, later Lady Dacre (whose spangled dress had provided the inspiration for 'She walks in beauty like the night'):

Mrs. * * [Wilmot]'s tragedy was last night damned. They may bring it on again, and probably will; but damned it was, — not a word of the last act audible. I went (*malgré* that I ought to have staid at home in sackcloth for unc., but I could not resist the *first* night of any thing) to a private and quiet nook of my private box, and witnessed the whole process. The first three acts, with transient gushes of applause, oozed patiently but heavily on. I must say it was badly acted, particularly by * * [Kean], who was groaned upon in the third act, — something about 'horror — such a horror' was the cause. Well, the fourth act became as muddy and turbid as need be; but the fifth — what Garrick used to call (like a fool) the *concoction* of a play — the fifth act stuck fast at the King's prayer. You know he says 'he never went to bed without saying them, and did not like to omit them now.' But he was no sooner upon his knees, than the audience got upon their legs — the damnable pit — and roared, and groaned, and hissed, and whistled. Well that was choked a little; but the ruffian-scene — the penitent peasantry — and killing the Bishop and the Princess — oh, it was all over. The curtain fell upon unheard actors, and the announcement attempted by Kean for Monday was equally ineffectual. Mrs. Bartley was so frightened, that, though the people were tolerably quiet, the Epilogue was quite inaudible to half the house.[107]

Byron drew several conclusions. First, *Ina* was 'not an *acting* play'; it had 'good language but no power'. Secondly, and much less justifiably, he allowed himself to deduce that 'Women (saving Joanna Baillie) cannot write tragedy; they have not seen enough nor felt enough of life for it'. Neither the sexist and patronizing generality of this verdict nor the more impartial critical assessment of an untheatrical tragedy should have deterred Byron from writing his own plays. Yet his account of the evening also suggests that, even if first nights were irresistible to a student of human behaviour, the vociferations of the 'damnable pit' and the humiliations of a public trial in unfavourable conditions were too dangerous to be risked. So Byron declares an end to theatrical ambition: 'It is . . . a good warning not to risk or write tragedies. I never had much bent that way; but, if I had, this would have cured me.' [108] The clarity and apparent firmness of this resolution take on a surprising ambivalence when viewed in the context of the rich dramatic output of Byron's later years. No doubt there is an element of Byronic inconsistency or 'mobility' in this apparent contradiction but Byron's experience at Drury Lane seems to have been one of the factors which disillusioned him with live theatre and an audience and propelled him towards the ideal conditions of what he later designated a 'mental theatre'. Recalling his time at Drury Lane, he told Thomas Medwin:

When I first entered upon theatrical affairs, I had some idea of writing for the house myself, but soon became a convert to Pope's opinion on that subject. Who would condescend to the drudgery of the stage, and enslave himself to the humours, the caprices, the taste or tastelessness, of the age? Besides, one must write for particular actors, have them continually in one's eye, sacrifice character to the personating of it, cringe to some favourite of the public, neither give him too many nor too few lines to spout, think how he would mouth such and such a sentence, look such and such a passion, strut such and such a scene. Who, I say, would submit to all this? [109]

Coleridge, it would seem, *was* prepared to make such compromises but Byron took as his warning the career of Shakespeare who had 'but little fame in his day' and whose plays had been so altered and corrupted over the years that it was no longer possible 'to separate what really is from what is not his own'. The strength of Byron's feeling is illustrated by an anecdote told by Walter Scott. When Scott declined Byron's invitation to write something for Drury Lane he included among his excuses for refusing 'the unpleasant yet necessary and inevitable subjection in which I must, as a dramatic writer, be necessarily kept by "the good folks in the green-room." *Caeteraque*, as I added, *ingenio non subeunda meo*. Byron sprang up and crossed the room with great vivacity, saying, "No, by G–, nor by mine either." ' [110]

The Romantic Poet and the Stage

The effects of such close contact with theatrical realities can be traced through Byron's letters and journals, and their influence certainly helped to shape the dramatic experiments of his later years when he was living in Italy and had long been separated from contact with the English theatre. The exception is *Werner* which he began while he was at Drury Lane in 1815 and which he revised and completed in 1821; this conventional and melodramatic piece was the most successful of his plays on the Victorian stage where it was regularly performed between 1830 and 1861. This posthumous success is a clear and ironic indication of the strength of those very tendencies which most of Byron's later plays were intended to escape or to transcend. The prevailing 'postulates' were frequently in his mind. *Marino Faliero*, for instance, is defined in his Journal in terms of what it is *not*:

... it is not intended for the stage. It is too regular — the time, twenty-four hours — the change of place not frequent — nothing *melo*-dramatic — no surprises, no starts, nor trap-doors, nor opportunities 'for tossing their heads and kicking their heels' — and no *love* — the grand ingredient of a modern play.[111]

In a letter to John Murray he admitted that his critics might be right in suggesting that his talent was *'essentially undramatic'* but defended himself by insisting on the essential tawdriness of the criteria for popular success in the theatre:

If M. F. don't fall — in the perusal — I shall perhaps try again — (but not for the Stage) and as I think that *love* is not the principal passion for tragedy — (& yet most of ours turns upon it) — you will not find me a popular writer. — Unless it is Love — *furious* — *criminal* — and *hapless* — it ought not to make a tragic subject — when it is melting & maudlin — it *does* — but it ought not to do — it is then for the Gallery — and second price boxes.[112]

In another letter he mixes some positive ideals with a catalogue of the dramatic ingredients of character and of plot which he has deliberately excluded:

— — And there are neither rings — nor mistakes — nor starts — nor outrageous ranting villains — nor melodrame in it. — All this will prevent it's popularity, but does not persuade me that it is *therefore* faulty. Whatever faults it has will arise from deficiency in the conduct — rather than in the conception — which is simple and severe.[113]

The emphasis on simplicity and severity is a recurrent feature of his letters where he also invokes the principle of austerity which seems to be both an antidote to popular criteria and a reaction against their excesses. The 'damnable pit', the gallery and the second-price boxes all drove him towards the dramatic unities and towards a set of standards which were strikingly unfashionable. Yet for all the puritanical resolutions and the devotion to classical models beyond the reach of the multitude, Byron's strongly articulated contempt for theatrical success may have concealed a complex of feelings and ideas which were much more enigmatic. His letters show that he had established an insurance policy against the possibility of failure which was apparently comprehensive:

> As to tragedy, I may try one day — but *never* for the *stage* — don't you see I have no luck there? — my two addresses were not liked — & my Committee-ship did but get me into scrapes — no — no — I shall not tempt the Fates that way — besides I should risk more than I could gain — I have no right to encroach on other men's ground — even if I could maintain my own. — You tell me that Maturin's second tragedy has failed — is not this an additional warning to everybody as well as to me — however if the whim seized me I should not consider that nor anything else — but the fact is that success on the stage is not to me an object of ambition — & I am not sure that it would please me to triumph — although it would doubtless vex me to fail. — For these reasons I never will put it to the test. — Unless I could beat them all — it would be nothing — & who could do that? nor I nor any man — the Drama is complete already — there can be nothing like what has been.[114]

From this we might reasonably deduce that Byron wanted to remove himself as securely as he could from any kind of competitive pressure: he did not wish to engage with an audience or to compete with contemporaries who were less gifted or less scrupulous and therefore more likely to succeed. Nor did he wish to enter the lists with Shakespeare or the Jacobean dramatists. 'The Drama is complete already' gives a splendidly unequivocal formulation to the anxiety of influence and to the feeling that original achievement was no longer possible, yet in the case of Byron it led in part at least not to an abdication of dramatic enterprise but to the pursuit of an ideal which was very different: 'I admire the old English dramatists — but this is quite another field — & has nothing to do with theirs. — I want to make a *regular* English drama — no matter whether for the Stage or not — which is not my object — but a *mental* theatre'.[115] Here the models (or, more properly the pioneers) were the Greek dramatists and their more recent followers such as Alfieri. In committing himself to such an initiative Byron was not only releasing himself from the eristic impulse, the desire to 'beat them all' but he was also liberating his verse from the Shakespearean resonances which weaken some of his other plays and which irreparably damage the work of most of his contemporaries. He would not succumb to the promptings of plot or to the requirements of spectacle (the prerequisites for popular success); nor would he yield to the loftier temptation to produce a poetic drama in the Shakespearean vein.

In the matter of language Byron here seems to be moving in a direction precisely opposite to that recommended by Keats. On reading *The Cenci*, Keats had sensed that Shelley had attempted to temper his style to the presumed taste of an audience at the cost of 'the Poetry, and dramatic effect'; in his view that was an unhappy compromise and he advised Shelley to ' "load every rift" of your subject with ore'.[116] Such Spenserean exuberance was foreign to Byron's taste and to his emerging view of the drama. For all his delighted knowledge of Shakespeare's plays, he had serious doubts about their poetic qualities; he once told Medwin that many of the comedies were 'insufferable to read, much more to see'. It was his intention to produce a poetic drama which avoided everything that was obviously 'poetic': 'But what has poetry to do with a play, or in a play? There is not one passage in Alfieri strictly poetical; hardly one in Racine.'[117] In comments such as these one can detect an element of exaggeration, of special pleading, perhaps; certainly, as Byron must have known, there is no lack of the poetic in the plays of Aeschylus, Sophocles and Euripides. And yet his instinct was a shrewd one and the achievement of *Marino Faliero* and *The Two Foscari* seems to show that he had discovered a mode which suited his own capacities and which was more truly dramatic in the austerity of its versification and in its ironic vision of history than the more obviously expressive attempts of many of his contemporaries. Byron claimed that *Marino Faliero* was '*not* a *political* play' and that it was 'purely Venetian' in its reference but the censorship which was exercised at Drury Lane makes it clear that to some readers at least its wider political resonances seemed all too threatening in the year after Peterloo.[118]

The case is an interesting one since it seems clear that in some senses the play was generated by an opposition to the practices of the contemporary stage. Yet, in escaping from such vitiating influences, Byron also elected to write a play which was calculatedly untheatrical: 'they might as well act the Prometheus of Aeschylus', he told Murray.[119] As he pointed out, it ran to 3,500 lines when 'a good acting play should not exceed 1500 or 1800'. 'What audience', he asked Medwin with a satisfaction which was self-justifying, self-frustrating, 'will listen with any patience to a mere tirade of poetry, which stops the march of the action?'[120] Here, more pointedly than anywhere else perhaps, one can sense the paradoxical nature of the Romantic relationship with the stage; and here too one can admire the achievement but regret the wasted potential.

TWO:
THE DRAMAS OF BYRON

Giorgio Melchiori

When I accepted some time ago to give this talk I was relying on the fact that in the '60s I had been so fascinated by Byron's dramatic productions that I made them the subject of a course in the University of Turin. I have now looked up my notes after so many years and I find to my dismay that I am in deep disagreement with them. Not that the charm of those plays has waned; what has changed completely is my approach to drama, not only Byron's but also in respect of the whole theatrical tradition, Shakespeare included. I had been looking at plays simply as literature, while now I see them not as literary texts but as mere pretexts which are fully realized only in performance. This of course is rather embarrassing in the case of Byron who constantly maintained that his plays were *not* for performance. He had been on the committee of the most important London theatre in its time, Drury Lane, and protested that this experience had made him loathe the very idea of having a play of his performed on the stage: that is what he stated in so many words in the letter he wrote to his publisher John Murray on 15 February 1817, when offering for publication his very first dramatic production, *Manfred*.[1]

I find this embarrassment of mine most stimulating because it urges me to reconsider along new lines the whole question of the contribution of the romantic poets not to literature, but more specifically to the theatre. Now if by theatre we mean a collective experience, close communication and participation between stage and audience in the presentation of the inner reality of man in all its aspects (not excluding the social and even political ones) — which is how theatre was understood in Shakespeare's time and fortunately is again understood now — if this is theatre, then there was no theatre in England at least since the Licensing Act of

1737. The Act had introduced an appalling discrimination, recognising as *legitimate* theatre only those entertainments offered to an audience who went to the playhouse not so much to *see* and be involved in the play performed, as to *be seen* by their fellow spectators, or at most to assess the individual art of star performers (and there were no doubt great actors like David Garrick), or, at a lower level, to admire and wonder at the new developments of stage machinery and special effects.

Now this, the legitimate theatre, was the only kind of dramatic expression that Byron had come into touch with in his time, when on the Drury Lane Committee — this and the travesties of Shakespeare for the benefit of the great contemporary actors. By refusing to have his plays performed in that theatre, Byron, by nature a rebel against any form of legitimacy, was reacting as it could be expected from him. But his protest did not and could not take the form of a return to Elizabethan or Shakespearean theatre conditions, because those conditions had been completely lost sight of. The original texts of Shakespeare's plays (as distinct from those presented on the stage) had become simply Literature. Even Charles Lamb, who rightly claimed to have been 'the first to draw the public attention to the old English dramatists' in his *Specimens of English Dramatic Poets contemporary with Shakspeare*, published in 1808 — even Lamb at the same time maintained that a play like *King Lear* could not and should not be acted on the stage, but could and should be appreciated instead only by reading it in the quiet of one's study; and the same was true of all the other specimens he had enthusiastically as well as piously rescued from oblivion. It is not surprising therefore that Byron, while rejecting on the one hand the theatre of his own time, should on the other object also to Shakespeare, whose genius and style he admired and more or less consciously even imitated, but whom he considered a bad, a deleterious model to modern playwrights, in so much as he ignored the rules that literature had imposed on drama. In the Preface to *Sardanapalus* and *The Two Foscari* Byron was to write that with any departure from the 'unities' 'there may be poetry, but can be no drama'; and went on deploring 'the unpopularity of this notion' in the modern English theatre, pointing out that, not very long ago, it was 'the law of literature throughout the world, and is still so in the more civilised parts of it'.[2]

Byron must find a different way of contesting the current legitimate theatre. This is what I propose to suggest, taking, I think, a different view from the current one on the meaning itself of Byron's dramas, and on the reasons for considering them not — as is generally done — either idiosyncratic or harking back to past models, but rather as essentially innovative, and, in many ways, modern — far ahead of their time. So that I shall look for terms of reference rather to our century and even to our contemporaries, than to his own or, Heaven forbid, to his predecessors, great as they may have been.

But let me first remind you of a few facts and data.

One: all Byron's dramas were written *after* he had left England for good, when he had severed all connections with the legitimate theatre of London and Drury Lane. This, I think, is in itself significant.

Two: they were written in Italy (even if the first of them was conceived in Switzerland), a country that gave Byron not only that wealth of sensual pleasures that everybody pretends to deplore, but also a different outlook on life, on interpersonal relationships, extending to the social field and the political.

Three: when in Italy, he stopped writing the sort of poems, the verse tales, that had given him the greatest fame and contributed so much to the creation of the mythical projection of his personality, the Byronic hero. The poems of Italian inspiration, like *The Lament of Tasso*, *The Prophecy of Dante*, show a completely different mood, and so, in another way, does that more delightful of his tales, *Beppo, a Venetian Story*, a happy prelude to at least one aspect of his unfinished masterpiece, *Don Juan*. The third canto of *Childe Harold*, begun in Switzerland and completed in Venice, lost the character of a travelogue shared by the first two, acquiring rather that of a more private reflection, though it must be acknowledged that the last, the Italian fourth canto, tries to meet the expectations of an English audience who had appreciated the first two parts of the poem as a kind of spiritual guidebook. But what we must keep in mind most is that all his dramas but one were written concurrently with his major work, *Don Juan*.

The dramas that Byron wrote are altogether eight, two of which he left, I think deliberately, unfinished. The word 'dramas' is in fact inadequate: he actually took great care in labelling each of them in a more appropriate way. The first of them, *Manfred*, written in 1816-17, he called 'A Dramatic Poem'. All the rest he composed within four years, between 1820 and 1825. This gap between the first and the rest of his plays is important; so much so that *Manfred* is generally seen as the conclusion of a poetic phase, while *Marino Faliero* marks the real beginning of Byron as a dramatist. I believe that this view must be modified, and we shall see why later. In fact the first idea of *Marino Faliero* came very close in time to *Manfred*. In a letter to his publisher John Murray of April 2, 1817, a letter in which Byron asks whether Murray has received the entire text of *Manfred*, he discusses the merits of Otway's *Venice Preserved*, and then goes on:

but the story of Marino Falieri — is different — & I think so much finer, — that I wish Otway had taken it instead; — the head conspiring against the body — for refusal of redress for a real injury; — jealousy, treason — with the more fixed and inveterate passions (mixed with policy) of an old or elderly man — the Devil himself could not have a finer subject — & he is your only tragic dramatist.[3]

At this stage Byron saw the subject merely as a missed opportunity for Otway and had no idea of writing a drama about it himself; it took him quite a while to convince himself that he could supply Otway's place, and for a time he thought of presenting that of the Venetian Doge as a private tragedy:

It is now four years that I have meditated this work; and before I had sufficiently examined the records, I was rather disposed to have made it turn on a jealousy in Faliero. But, perceiving no foundation for this in historical truth, and aware that jealousy is an exhausted passion in the drama, I have given it a more historical form.[4]

This he wrote in the long preface to the play, adding:

I have had no view to the stage; in its present state it is, perhaps, not a very exalted object of ambition; besides I have been too much behind the scenes to have thought it so at any time. And I cannot conceive any man of irritable feeling putting himself at the mercies of an audience. The sneering reader, and the loud critic, and the tart review, are scattered and distant calamities; but the trampling of an intelligent or of an ignorant audience on a production which, be it good or bad, has been a mental labour to the writer, is a palpable and immediate grievance, heightened by a man's doubt of their competency to judge, and his certainty of his own imprudence in electing them his judges. Were I capable of writing a play which could be deemed stage-worthy, success would give me no pleasure and failure great pain. It is for this reason that, even during the time of being one of the committee of one of the theatres, I never made the attempt, and never will.[5]

It is in a way a candid statement, the obvious implication being that, disgusted with what was called theatre in his own time, Byron was writing for a yet unborn type of theatre, a theatre of the future of which he could not envisage the advent, and that is why he called it later a 'theatre of the mind'. His definition of *Marino Faliero* was 'An Historical Tragedy'. The same definition he used for *The Two Foscari*, which appeared next year together with *Sardanapalus*. The latter he described simply as a tragedy, and in the preface to the two works he insisted that they were not composed 'with the most remote view to the stage'.[6] For *Cain*, instead, which also appeared in the same year, he used the subtitle 'A Mystery', 'in conformity', as he explains in the Preface, 'with the ancient title annexed to dramas upon similar subjects, which were styled "Mysteries, or Moralities" '.[7] In this case the awareness that the chosen subject, and especially his treatment of it in making Cain the hero rather than the villain, might give offence, prompts a disclaimer based on the subtitle itself:

The author has by no means taken the same liberties with his subject which were common formerly, as may be seen by any reader curious enough to refer to those very profane productions, whether in English, French, Italian, or Spanish.[8]

And a further justification is felt necessary for the language used, especially in the case of Lucifer:

With regard to the language of Lucifer, it was difficult for me to make him talk like a clergyman on the same subjects; but I have done what I could to restrain him within the bounds of spiritual politeness.[9]

Shortly after *Cain* Byron undertook the writing of another mystery, and in this case the choice of subject was a deliberate challenge: it is based on a controversial passage of *Genesis* to which Byron had already referred in *Manfred*: 'And it came to pass that the Sons of God saw the daughters of men that they were fair; and they took them wives of all which they chose'.[10] This was taken to refer to the loves of the angels with earthly women from which a race of giants had been born, as Manfred says:

> the vigorous race
> Of undiseased mankind, the giant sons
> Of the embrace of angels with a sex
> More beautiful than they . . .[11]

The mystery, entitled *Heaven and Earth*, is deliberately lyrical in mood, experimenting in a number of stanzaic forms that suggest a musical rather than a literary pattern. It is the shortest of Byron's plays, and the reason given for this brevity is its unfinished state. Byron published the two scenes in Leigh Hunt's periodical *The Liberal* in Pisa as the first part of a work in progress that he would complete only after seeing what kind of reaction it met with. The fact is that the scene of the outbreak of the deluge with the destruction of mankind while Noah's ark sails on the waters and the angels fly away to unknown interstellar spaces with their woman lovers, is a grandiose conclusion to a story that cannot have any further development. I believe that *Heaven and Earth* was actually conceived as the representation of a mystery, and as such it was meant from the beginning to present no solution; its message is in its lack of conclusion: Byron had conceived it as an open work.

It is somehow surprising to find, immediately after *Heaven and Earth*, the most elaborate and sensational of Byron's 'tragedies' bearing a traditional title: *Werner; or, the Inheritance*. It is conceived in the style of the more orthodox Gothic tales, and in fact Byron acknowledges that it is based on a sensational story called 'The German's Tale, Kruitzner', which he had read in a popular collection when he was a boy of fourteen. He explains:

> I had begun a drama upon this tale so far back as 1815 (the first I ever attempted, except one at thirteen years old, called 'Ulric and Ilvina', which I had sense enough to burn), and had nearly completed an act, when I was interrupted by circumstances.[12]

But the most interesting remark about this sensational story is Byron's avowal that 'The German's Tale' 'may indeed be said to contain the germ of much that I have since written'.[13] It is a revealing acknowledgement of Byron's consciousness of the waywardness of the creative process. Surely the anonymous original story translated or adapted from an even more obscure source had no particular literary merit. It was exploiting all the commonplaces of a *genre* which was fast losing all pretence at literary dignity. By pointing to it as 'the germ of much' of his later work, of whose merit he had no doubt, Byron is suggesting that the work of art is not the result of a mysterious inspiration from above, but springs from a common ground, part and parcel of everyday experience in reading as in writing. There is definite defiance in his next remark: 'I merely refer the reader to the original story, that he may see to what extent I have borrowed from it; and I am not unwilling that he should find much greater pleasure in perusing it than the drama which is founded upon its contents'.[14] Actually *Werner* was the only play by Byron that was successful on the stage during the nineteenth century: its highly melodramatic tone and the opportunities it offered for conventional histrionics suited the tastes of the audiences of exactly that theatre that Byron deplored. But, with the advent of the new awareness of the proper function of the theatre, it was again forgotten. Byron's dramas that have instead survived into this century, but for very different reasons, are those that lend themselves to being turned into something else. I have used the words 'melodramatic tone' for *Werner*. Melodrama, if taken in its original meaning and not simply as a derogatory epithet, is a key for the understanding of these survivals. Verdi has transformed *Marino Faliero* and *The Two Foscari* into operas that still hold the stage, while Schumann's *Manfred* in oratorio form, with a *voce recitante* taking the role of the hero, can still be a very exciting theatrical experience. And the more so if the actor taking Manfred's part is not afraid of abandoning himself to the most blatant vocal histrionics, like Carmelo Bene a couple of years ago in a memorable performance at the Rome opera.

Now this should give us pause. Why should *Manfred* lend itself to and come alive under such treatment? Let us turn to Byron's text and take a closer look. *Manfred*, as I stated earlier, was taken formerly to be the final expression of the Byronic hero, transgression personified, the ultimate romantic ideal, the fatal man described by Mario Praz as the last metamorphosis of Satan. Now this is largely true. But should we take these definitions in dead seriousness? Should we approach him as a clinical case to whom the most refined tests of modern psychological science can be rewardingly applied? Let us look at the text. We are immediately informed:

The Scene of the Drama is amongst the Higher Alps . . . Act I, Scene i.
MANFRED *alone.* — *Scene, a Gothic gallery.* — *Time, Midnight.*
> The lamp must be replenish'd, but even then
> It will not burn so long as I must watch:
> My slumbers — if I slumber — are not sleep,
> But a continuance of enduring thought,
> Which then I can resist not: in my heart
> There is a vigil, and these eyes but close
> To look within; and yet I live, and bear
> The aspect and the form of breathing men.
> But grief should be the instructor of the wise;
> Sorrow is knowledge: they who know the most
> Must mourn the deepest o'er the fatal truth,
> The Tree of Knowledge is not that of Life.
> Philosophy and science, and the springs
> Of wonder, and the wisdom of the world,
> I have essay'd, and in my mind there is
> A power to make these subject to itself —
> But they avail not: I have done men good,
> And I have met with good even among men —
> But this avail'd not: I have had my foes,
> And none have baffled, many fallen before me —
> But this avail'd not: — Good, or evil, life,
> Powers, passions, all I see in other beings,
> Have been to me as rain unto the sands,
> Since that all-nameless hour. I have no dread,
> And feel the curse to have no natural fear,
> Nor fluttering throb, that beats with hopes or wishes,
> Or lurking love of something on the earth.[15]

The echoes of Doctor Faustus's opening monologue in Marlowe's play are obvious. They are actually so deliberate, and the evocation of a medley of seven spirits in the following lines is so highfalutin' that a suspicion begins to emerge in my mind. A suspicion reinforced by the Gothic gallery as a background and the midnight hour mentioned in the stage direction. I cannot help feeling that there is a strong element of parody in all this set-up. In order to test this uneasy feeling I turned to the available statements of Byron about *Manfred*. The most obvious is the letter to John Murray of 15 February 1817, when he had just finished writing the play. And here we find:

I forgot to mention to you — that a kind of poem in dialogue (in blank verse) or drama . . . is finished — it is in three acts — but of a very wild — metaphysical — and inexplicable kind. — Almost all the persons —

but two or three — are Spirits of the earth & air — or the waters — the scene is in the Alps — the hero a kind of magician who is tormented by a species of remorse — the cause of which is left half unexplained — he wanders about invoking these spirits — which appear to him — & are of no use — he at last goes to the very abode of the Evil principle in propria persona — to evocate a ghost — which appears — & gives him an ambiguous & disagreeable answer — & in the 3d. act he is found by his attendants dying in a tower — where he studied his art.[16]

Incidentally, this is an admirable synthetic summary of the play, and a fair one — but what about its tone? The letter, which I have quoted in part before, goes on to explain: 'you may perceive by this outline that I have no great opinion of this piece of phantasy', its only merit being, according to Byron, that of being unperformable.[17] A month later Byron wrote about *Manfred* to his friend the poet Thomas Moore (the author, incidentally, of a poem on *The Loves of the Angels* — see *Heaven and Earth*):

Almost all the *dram. pers.* are spirits, ghosts, or magicians, and the scene is in the Alps and the other world, so you may suppose what a Bedlam tragedy it must be.[18]

At this point I have no doubts: *Manfred*, this Bedlam tragedy, the Witch Drama, as Byron called it later in his correspondence with Murray, was a final revisitation of the Byronic hero conceived in a spirit of self-irony. I do not mean that he wrote it with his tongue in his cheek, as a laborious joke at the expense of the candid reader who would take it at its face value and be duly shocked by it. That of *Manfred* is a deeply tragic theme, entailing a total involvement of the author, who recognised in the hero's his own intimate plight. It has nothing in common with satire proper, that Byron had so ably handled in his earlier poetry; but neither does it share the single-minded earnestness of *The Giaour*, *The Corsair* or *Lara*. We must remember once again that the writing of *Manfred* was followed very closely by that of *Beppo*, the Venetian story, apparently the most light-hearted of Byron's works — but when he sent it to his publisher Byron advised him not to include it in the magazine that he edited but to print it separately, because 'it won't do for your journal — being full of political allusions'.[19] What I wish to suggest is that, improbable as it may look, *Manfred* and *Beppo* belong together: they mark a new mood, Byron's discovery of ambiguity as the essential quality of great poetry as well as great drama. In the same way as behind the amusing irony of *Beppo* and inextricably linked with it there is ferocity and politics, so behind the grandiloquent tragic self-searching of Manfred there is a constant ironical strain, a deliberate supererogation of feeling, that acts as mockery of the tragic. Mind you, I believe that there is nothing more serious than this kind of mockery and irony: it creates a double level of apprehension, in so much as the inner conflict between the playful, the ironical consciousness (what is now called the ludic element) and the highly dramatic becomes the very substance of a tragic view of life. Nobody was more conscious of it than that greatest of dramatists, Shakespeare: the jokes of the clown who brings the asp to Cleopatra, the indecent puns of Lear at the height of his madness are among the most obvious examples. They are not, as it was said at one time, comic relief: they bear witness to the inextricable tangle of human feelings and reactions which is the substance of tragedy. Goethe knew that Mephistophilis was a comedian (and Byron dedicated to Goethe as the author of *Faust* two of his tragedies, significantly the two that at first sight seem the least Faustian that he wrote), and Goethe had learned it from his model, Marlowe's *Doctor Faustus*, which, as we saw, Byron deliberately parodied in the opening scene of *Manfred*.

The real trouble with the legitimate theatre of the late eighteenth and early nineteenth century was the utter separation of the *genres*: tragedy being exclusively tragic from beginning to end (except perhaps for the obtrusive insertion of some clowning by low characters) and comedy had to be comic from beginning to end. What was lost was the sense — to put it in Yeats's words — that 'Hamlet and Lear are gay; / Gaiety transfiguring all that dread'.[20]

Reacting, as we saw, to the legitimate theatre, Byron found another way of breaking up the lifeless divisions it had established, of recovering the lost gaiety of tragedy: through self-irony, through parody, through transparent over-emphasis that acted as a deforming mirror of the inner reality, lending it the quality of the grotesque. He had models for it at hand. Why was melodrama — I mean Italian opera at its grandest — the most valid form of tragic theatre in the nineteenth century? Because the requirements — the intrusion — of the music, give a completely new dimension to the drama, introducing in the acting a palpable element of the grotesque that reacts against the commonplace and makes the world of feeling larger than life. And I suspect that when in 1821 Byron explained to John Murray that his 'dramatic system' was 'more like a play of Alfieri's than of your stage',[21] he was referring to the same sort of thing. The utterly unrealistic language and action of Alfieri's tragedies have the same powerful grotesque effect of grand opera. And Byron had experienced it personally: in August 1821 he wrote from Bologna:

Last night I went to the representation of Alfieri's *Mirra*, — the last two acts of which threw me into convulsions. — I do not mean by that word — a lady's hysterics — but the agony of reluctant tears — and the choaking shudder which I do not often undergo for fiction . . . The worst was that the *'dama'*, in whose box I was — went off in the same way — I really believe more from fright — than any other sympathy — at least with the players — but she has been ill — and I have been ill and we are all languid & pathetic this morning — with great expenditure of Sal Volatile.[22]

In this case the comic intrudes in the comment, but at the origin of it is the situation created by the theatrical *fiction* — a word emphasised by Byron. In a way Alfieri's, like opera, is theatre of the absurd, and it is exactly in the absurdity of it that the ludic element lay, or lies. What I wish to suggest is that we are wrong in approaching Byron's dramas in a mood of solemn seriousness, as expressions of profound psychological inner conflicts. Of course, there is also that, but there is as much deliberate grotesqueness, irony, sardonic deformation.

This tendency to approach works of fiction as solemn and humourless works of art to be sounded in depth, without suspecting that they may be or contain jokes at their own or our expense, prevents, I feel, a real appreciation of some of the greatest works of literature of our century. It is the case, for instance, of Joyce's major novels: *Ulysses* and *Finnegans Wake* are extremely serious, substantially tragic and deeply committed books, but from most of the highly appreciative criticism one reads of them it hardly appears that they are also masterpieces of humour deserving a place side by side with Byron's *Don Juan*. And surely this accounts for Joyce's sympathy with Byron. We have Stanislaus Joyce's word for the authenticity of the episode the novelist recounts in *A Portrait of the Artist as a Young Man* when as a boy in the Jesuit College at Clongowes he was discussing with fellow pupils the best English writers. As the best prose writer he indicated Cardinal Newman, meeting with the approval of the others; but when it came to the best poet the other boys agreed on the name of Tennyson, he countered with 'Byron, of course'. The others 'joined in a scornful laugh'; one said that Byron was 'a heretic and immoral too', another that he was 'a bad man', at which they all got hold of him and started hitting him and forcing him against a barbed wire fence, shouting:

— Admit that Byron was no good.
— No.
— Admit.
— No.
— Admit.
— No. No.
At last after a fury of plunges he wrenched himself free. His tormentors set off . . . laughing and jeering at him, while he, torn and flushed and panting, stumbled after them half blinded with tears, clenching his fists madly and sobbing.[23]

That this was no youthful infatuation is confirmed by the fact that in later life, when in Paris in 1930-31 Joyce wanted to help the Irish tenor John Sullivan for whom he had the greatest admiration, he tried to convince the musician George Antheil to turn Byron's *Cain* into an opera; when asked by Antheil to rewrite the text in libretto form he replied 'I would never have the bad manners to rewrite the text of a great English poet', but offered to lend his name as adapter of the text by judicious cutting, commenting 'I am quite content to go down to posterity as a scissor and paste man'.[24] Unfortunately nothing came of the project; but Joyce's intuition of Byron's melodramatic genius is evidence enough of a deeper affinity.

But there is another feature of Byron's dramas that reveals them as surprisingly modern. In spite of the exasperated individualism of their heroes, all Byron's dramas, to use the words with which he defined *Beppo*, have politics and ferocity, that is to say a strong ideological commitment and as strong a streak of cruelty. These are elements hardly present in the theatre of his time, while they are, I should say, endemic — and fortunately so — in that of ours. At their best and most powerful, commitment, cruelty and, emphatically, the grotesque characterise the works of an author that I consider the one great English tragic dramatist of our time, Edward Bond. Stylistically he and Byron seem poles apart, and it may well be that Bond has never read Byron's dramas; but in fact their motivations, their approach to the function of drama, their constant echoes and parodies of the Elizabethans, the ironical emphasis of the tragic action is identical. Should we say that Byron is the Bond of his time or that Bond is the Byron of our time?

I have mentioned up to now only seven of the eight dramas that Byron wrote; I have left out the last because it is extremely indicative of the road that Byron the dramatist was going to take. The title itself of this play is extraordinary: *The Deformed Transformed* — and in this case the author could not find for it any better definition than 'A Drama'. Not a tragedy, or a history or a mystery, but a mixture of them all. The Advertisement warns us:

> This production is founded partly on the story of a novel called 'The Three Brothers', published many years ago, from which M. G. Lewis's 'Wood Demon' was also taken; and partly on the 'Faust' of the great Goethe. The present publication contains the two first Parts only, and the opening chorus of the third. The rest may perhaps appear hereafter.[25]

In fact it did not. Byron died in Missolonghi shortly after the publication. The action moves freely in time and space from a German forest to the walls of Rome besieged by mercenaries fighting for the Constable of Bourbon, from inside St. Peter's to 'a Castle in the Appennines surrounded by a wild but smiling Country'.[26] The autobiographical note is sounded from the very first lines, when a cruel mother insults her lame and deformed son (Byron had always resented deeply his mother's scorn because he was slightly lame). A mysterious stranger appears to the boy Arnold and, with an incantation, in exchange for his soul, gives Arnold the shape of Achilles while the demon himself assumes Arnold's deformed body and the name of Caesar. They join the Bourbon at the siege of Rome. Here, quite casually, there is a brief fight between Arnold and Benvenuto Cellini, who has just shot dead the Constable of Bourbon. Shortly after in St. Peter's the soldiers assault the Pope, with the Demon Caesar as cheer-leader:

> Now, Priest! Now, soldier! the two great professions
> Together by the ears and hearts! I have not
> Seen a more comic pantomime since Titus
> Took Jewry.[27]

And in fact the whole thing *is* a comic pantomime, as when Olimpia Colonna jumps on the main altar and, embracing a massive crucifix, casts it down on a soldier who tries to reach her and kills him. When Arnold arriving asks why the soldiers want to kill her one replies:

> Count, she hath slain our comrade.
> *Arnold*   With what weapon?
> *Soldier* The cross, beneath which he is crush'd; behold him
>   Lie there, more like a worm than man; she cast it
>   Upon his head.[28]

The play could ramble on like this for ever, interspersed with songs, incantations, and choruses of soldiers, citizens and spirits, but it suddenly stops after a chorus of peasants which is supposed to begin the third part, before the gates of a castle in the Appennines. How far had Byron planned its continuation? We shall never know. What we know is that Byron in 1823 was already writing a play that could be indifferently claimed by the theatre of the grotesque, the theatre of cruelty and the theatre of the absurd. No mean achievement for his time.

THREE:
SHELLEYAN DRAMA

Stuart Curran

In discussing Romantic drama, we labour under two problems, both of which are to some extent historically determined. The first is that we do not believe in it; the second that we do not believe that it deserves to be considered as a separate entity. Until, as with this series of essays, we are asked directly to confront Byron's remarkable commitment to drama in his later years, or to honour Shelley's intense interest in dramatic composition, we tend to look for, and to talk and write on, other subjects. More is usually made of Keats's desire to write drama than on Byron and Shelley's actual achievements in the form. I think this is so, because we have, even if unintentionally, adopted a view of the Romantic period that is untrue to it, that, indeed, is often defined by the distortions of Victorian poets and critics, who were compelled to create for themselves a vital presence to replace the vacuum that they inherited. The apparently sudden disappearance of an entire generation of young, brilliant, visionary poets is without parallel in the entire history of European poetry. Whereas in Italy and France the 1820s and '30s saw the true birth of a new and nationalistic poetry, and with it a startling renewal of the powers of their language and heritage, the poets of Britain faced an acute sense of curtailment. Tennyson was a mere fourteen years Keats's junior, but where was the Keats the youthful poet tried to recreate in his verse? Twenty years separated Browning from Shelley, but it might as well have been a gulf. Not that these and other aspiring voices of the early 1830s did not regard their predecessors with awe; the very absence of those kindred voices, paradoxically, created a presence far more intimidating than that of Coleridge, or Southey, or Wordsworth, still alive in 1830 but moribund in poetic spirit, perhaps safely so from the perspective of the new generation.

The relationship of the Younger Romantics and early Victorians is perhaps the classic case of what Harold Bloom has called the anxiety of influence, though it is less personal than cultural and generational. Keats learned at his brother's bedside that we do not live in art, yet, by an irony that is almost too perfect, he became for Tennyson the model aesthete from whom the younger poet weaned himself through the long tutelage of his own grief over Hallam. The case of Browning is even starker in its outlines and of great importance for the present inquiry. For his rewriting of Shelley determined the standard view of the poet among the Victorians and still persists, if weakened by the inevitable assault of the actual, today. Browning's 'Sun-treader', the epitome of visionary lyricism, was easily translated into Arnold's 'ineffectual angel'. With Shelley constellated among the stars, there was considerable room for the gruff Browning to tread the solid earth and peer into the psychological depths of a cast of almost too real *dramatis personae*. And yet, there are times for Browning — the clear debt of *The Ring and the Book* to *The Cenci* is the greatest example — when the long-observed fiction threatens to break down. But he did not have to rely only on himself to sustain it: among others there was John Stuart Mill, rigorously demanding that poetry concern itself with feeling and novels with fact and simultaneously celebrating Shelley as the purest of lyric models. It is true that Shelley can approach closer than any other British Romantic to the delicate, limpid lieder we associate with German Romanticism. But the great bulk of what he himself published before his death is narrative and dramatic. His recasting by a later generation is actually a symptom of a large cultural revision whose conceptions still colour our attitudes today. The fact is that Romanticism as a term literally comes from the revival of medieval romance that was undertaken throughout western Europe at the end of the eighteenth century. The paradox could not be more sharply drawn: in talking about the 'romantic', we say narrative and think lyric. Richard Hurd, at the beginning of that revival of romance, ended his seminal book by warning his age that in the pursuit of dry fact 'we have lost a world of fine fabling': doubtless, he would be pleased to know that the fabling persists.

But rather than linger over these paradoxes, let me revert to some dry facts of our own that indicate the remarkable extent of

Shelley's interest in drama. It appears to have been whetted by two periods of residence in London, in January and February of 1817, during the Chancery suit over custody of his children, and particularly a year later, just before the Shelleys left England for Italy. At the time, at least as Peacock remembered it forty years later, the poet was less interested in drama *per se* than he was in acting, especially the mercurial intensity of the new school of Romantic acting embodied in Edmund Kean and Eliza O'Neill.[1] They were the models around whom a year later in Italy he conceived and wrote *The Cenci*, the tragedy on which rests his reputation as a dramatist of great promise and this single success. But if we enlarge our view a little, I think that we can recognize that drama, at least dramatic situation, was on his mind virtually from the point he arrived in Italy: he describes himself in the Preface to *The Cenci* as 'one whose attention has but newly been awakened to the study of dramatic literature'.

Newly awakened he was. When Maria Gisborne first showed him the account of the Cenci family in Livorno, he immediately saw its dramatic possibilities and suggested it as such to Mary. It was sometime during this period that he likewise proposed to Mary the reign of Charles the First as a subject for tragedy. Even before setting forth to recast Aeschylean tragedy in the late summer of 1818 Shelley had undertaken his first major effort in translation from the Greek, the *Symposium* of Plato. This has been understood to signal the beginning of the Neoplatonic phase in his thought; but a moment's contemplation should suggest not only how inappropriate to Neoplatonic dogma is such a work, with its five (perhaps with the entrance of Alcibiades, six) conflicting views on the nature of love, but also that of all the dialogues of Plato the *Symposium* is the most inherently dramatic. The third major project from the Greek was undertaken the next year, and, though the evidence is skimpy, would appear to have been done during the revision of *The Cenci* and *Prometheus Unbound*: a translation of Euripides' *Cyclops*, the only surviving satyr play from the Athenian stage. It may be significant — at least it is unusual given the normal picture of Shelley — that *The Cyclops* is high comedy, not quite as ludicrous as Aristophanes' conception (in the *Symposium*) of primordial human beings as androgynous eggs, but sharing the same zany sense of humour. But the account of 1818-1819 does not stop here. For while Shelley was writing *The Cenci* in the summer of 1819 he was also studying Spanish with Maria Gisborne and beginning his series of translations from Calderón de la Barca, who would later become perhaps the crucial influence on his notions of drama.

That influence is first indelibly felt in 1819 and, I would suggest, in a very curious and unexpected place, *The Mask of Anarchy*, in which the superimposition of contending realities and the sense of politics as public spectacle all reduce in a play on words to a metaphorical pun, the theatrical masque as mask, which — in modern critical parlance — is pure metadrama. Shelley was also reading seventeenth-century English drama, including its principal masques, in the autumn of 1819; and he knew quite well, and I have argued elsewhere was deliberately playing against, the major example of the masque form among contemporary British poets, Leigh Hunt's *The Descent of Liberty* of 1815.[2] That *The Mask of Anarchy* is not rendered in dramatic form should not blind us to the extent that it is conceived in terms of drama, drama both as a genre and, in the larger sense, as objective representation. Moreover, if we extend this notion, the notion of dramatic objectivity, or that literary attitude we recognize as inherently dramatic, we will observe that two other major poetic efforts of this period also fall within our view. The first is *Rosalind and Helen, a Modern Ecloque*, rather a failure for all its 1300 lines, and second, a poem whose great success may have been conditioned by the earlier failure, *Julian and Maddalo, a Conversation*. I quote the subtitles of these poems to indicate that Shelley explicitly placed both works within the rubric of dialogue.

To sum up my argument thus far, in his first year and a half in Italy Shelley wrote two dramas, *Prometheus Unbound* and *The Cenci*, translated the whole of Euripides' *Cyclops*, began to translate Calderón, translated as well the most dramatic of the *Dialogues* of Plato, the *Symposium*, conceived two major poems as dialogues resisting reductive closure, and wrote a stirring political call for action juxtaposing action and spectacle in a sophisticated understanding of the traditions of the masque. I will concede that 'Lines Written among the Euganean Hills' is not a drama, but its isolation among Shelley's major efforts during this period only places in relief his absorption in the nature, the meaning, the creation of drama.

Something comparable, if not equal in achievement, happens with Shelley after he settled in Pisa, particularly in his last year there. As early as the summer of 1820, however, Shelley found it natural (though he is unique among the British Romantics in this) to revert to the style and mode of Aristophanes in order to couch his satire, *Swellfoot the Tyrant*, on the political milieu of the divorce trial of Queen Caroline, in a dramatic form. One might immediately suppose that the decisive event in Shelley's concentrated return to the drama in his last year would be Byron's arrival in Pisa. Yet, perhaps it is more accurate to suggest that it was actually Byron's delay in leaving Ravenna, where he was finishing *Sardanapalus* and writing *Cain* and *Heaven and Earth*, that gave Shelley a comparative freedom to write in the form. He had *Hellas* virtually complete and had begun *Charles the First* well before Byron at last appeared and settled into the Palazzo Lanfranchi. Again, the same pattern we witnessed in 1818-1819 occurs. It is not just that Shelley is writing drama, he is also actively engaged in its translation, first *El Mágico Prodigioso* of Calderón, plus scenes from others of his plays, then Goethe's *Faust*. We also have the curious 'Fragment of an Indian Drama' from this period, which appears to have been an attempt to adapt the perfumed, fantastic, and amorous atmosphere of the *Sakuntala* of Kalidasa, the classic Sanscrit drama, to English verse. As usual, Shelley throws his net very wide.

One difference from the initial year in Italy is that Shelley is not alone in his thespian pursuits. Indeed, the entire Pisan Circle seems to have been engaged in them. Mary Shelley wrote *Proserpine, a Mythological Drama* while in Pisa, though it was not published until 1832, in the Christmas annual, *Winter's Wreath*. Shelley contributed a brief hymn to that drama; and he also wrote several versions of an epithalamion for a play by Edward Williams, called *The Promise; or, A Year, a Month and a Day*. And it seems almost certain that Shelley's translations from *Faust* were the impetus for Byron's second attempt, the first being *Manfred*, to appropriate (or misappropriate) Goethe's drama: *The Deformed Transformed*, which he began that winter in Pisa. Once Byron appeared on the scene — or perhaps it was that *deux ex machina* Trelawny — it was no longer simply dramaturgy that interested the circle, but theatrics as well. The spring carnival masquerade in 1822 featured Mary Shelley in Turkish garb and Jane Williams in Indian, and another night the two were joined at a fancy dress ball by Edward Williams and Trelawny. Lest we dismiss Shelley as a mere stay-at-home, we should perhaps recall the amateur performance of *Othello* planned by the circle. In our amusement over the typecasting of Byron as Iago, the warrior Trelawny as Othello, or Mary as Desdemona we forget the salient fact that the director was to have been Shelley. Two further documents from this year need to be added to the list: one, dating from after Byron's arrival, is the curious dialogue, 'Byron and Shelley on the Character of Hamlet', whose basic authenticity is accepted, even though its authorship remains uncertain. The other piece has only recently come to light: Shelley's review in Italian of the performance of the Improvvisatore Tommaso Sgricci, whose quasi-classical tragedy on the death of Hector, in which he played all the parts — there appear to have been ten, including the chorus — was given in Pisa on the 22nd of January 1821. This was actually the third such virtuoso performance by Sgricci witnessed by Shelley, and Paul Dawson's supposition that these improvised classical tragedies, with their interpolated choruses, influenced the nature and form of *Hellas* — called by Shelley in his preface 'a mere improvise' — is surely right.[3] Indeed, when we place Mary Shelley's classical and mythological drama *Proserpine* in the same balance, we might wish to credit these performances with sparking the renewal of Shelley's interest in drama after a year's hiatus.

And yet, perhaps, I am splitting hairs in establishing two distinct periods for Shelley's interest in drama: in our retrospect, once he arrived in Italy that 'newly awakened' interest was both intense and generally sustained, resulting in four complete works in dramatic form, two others left unfinished, a number of narrative poems employing dramatic techniques and metaphors, and dramatic translations from three languages. The clearest evidence of the continuity of Shelley's interest has yet to be mentioned: these are the paragraphs on drama in *A Defence of Poetry*, written in the spring of 1821. I have delayed their introduction so as first to present the evidence for what might seem an uncharacteristic stance for Shelley, his celebration of drama as the highest form of literature. And yet that celebration is entirely characteristic in its recognition of the social context and purpose of art: 'the connexion of poetry and social good is more observable in the drama than in whatever other form: and it is indisputable that the highest perfection of human society has ever corresponded with the highest dramatic excellence'.[4] Shelley goes on in this passage to compare the dramatist to popular notions of providence, which recalls a similar assertion made with ringing authority in his preface to *The Cenci* two years earlier: 'Imagination is as the immortal God which should assume flesh for the redemption of mortal passion'.[5]

Elsewhere in the *Defence* and in his letters Shelley echoes Tasso's celebration of the epic poet, in his *Discorsi del Poema Eroico*, for creating a heterocosm of God's universe: 'Non merita nome di creatore, se non Iddio ed il poeta.' But as admiring of epic poetry as Shelley is, it is ultimately not the quasi-divine conceptual power of the imagination that he places first, but its incarnation 'for the redemption of mortal passion'. 'The highest moral purpose aimed at in the highest species of the drama, is the teaching the human heart, through its sympathies and antipathies, the knowledge of itself, in proportion to the possession of which knowledge, every human being is wise, just, sincere, tolerant and kind'.[6] My suspicion is that Shelley would rather have been Milton or Dante than Shakespeare or Sophocles; but at least for the purposes of defending poetry against Peacock's claim of its lack of utility, Shelley places above the capacity of the individual to imagine new worlds the nature of drama as a mirror revealing the inner soul of humanity.

> The drama, so long as it continues to express poetry, is as a prismatic and many-sided mirror, which collects the brightest rays of human nature and divides and reproduces them from the simplicity of these elementary forms, and touches them with majesty and beauty, and multiplies all that it reflects, and endows it with the power of propagating its like wherever it may fall.[7]

Or, again: 'The tragedies of the Athenian poets are as mirrors in which the spectator beholds himself, under a thin disguise of circumstance, stript of all but that ideal perfection and energy which every one feels to be the internal type of all that he loves, admires, and would become'.[8] These are noble sentiments, and at first sight this reiterated metaphor of the drama as mirror may seem little more than a restatement of Aristotelian mimesis, imitation. And yet, it is very different. Though certainly determined by the dramatic aesthetics of its own time, there are elements that are strikingly modern in Shelley's account of drama in his *Defence of Poetry*. I wish to concentrate on two as being the fundamental characteristics of Shelleyan drama. The one is that the mirror reflects not actions, as in Aristotle's formula for mimesis, but passions. The second is what is contained within that curious phrase, 'a prismatic and many-sided mirror'. Since both subjects are interrelated, I will not attempt an artificial separation.

Since we are talking about mirrors, let me, by way of illustrating how Shelley looks into them, turn things inside-out and begin at the end. Though Shelley found *Charles the First*, as he put it 'a devil of a nut . . . to crack', there are signs that the difficulty was not, as has been suggested, that he lacked sympathy for both his royal protagonists and Puritan antagonists, or that he could not discover a principle of action to impel the drama; but rather that, under the influence of Calderón, he was attempting to create a highly sophisticated drama that mirrored both the turbulence of the seventeenth century and its own reflection of it.[9] That is to say, *Charles the First* might be viewed as Shelley's most ambitious attempt yet to present a drama that looked continually into itself as into a mirror even as it represented itself to readers or auditors as a spectacle to contemplate and through which to contemplate themselves.

Its first scene returns to the underlying figure of *The Mask of Anarchy*, which Shelley was aware had never been published, to develop it dramatically. His several London citizens, representing a cross-section of a disaffected and potentially revolutionary public, converse against the backdrop of a triumphal procession. But it is not quite a triumph; rather, it is the makings of one. The various sets, engines, performers are being brought through the crowd to be assembled for a performance in Whitehall that takes place between the first and second scenes and from which this crowd will be wholly excluded. The king is introduced at the beginning of the second scene thanking all the participants, who have just concluded their masque. The self-congratulatory ritual of the masque presumes an order, a formal hierarchy, even a divine plan that is specious. The mirror into which Charles looks reflects what he wants to see in his interior chamber, not the reality of the citizens outdoors. The masque pointedly takes place off-stage, which might suggest, in this stage world of multiple illusion, that in some curious sense it never takes place at all. The masque is the ritualized mirror of Charles's divine right, his arbitrary authority, his self-mythologizing. In the real world, where the citizens converse, there are only bits and pieces of authority, painted backdrops, fragments of a fiction, illusions of an illusion. And yet as the citizens themselves recognize, these signs and symbols of power carry meaning even when unorganized: they are shams, but they serve a power with arbitrary — indeed, as the scenes of the play progress, with increasingly brutal — consequences to the lives and fortunes of the people.

It is in such a context that one of the citizens turns to a youth who is fascinated with the stage properties being carried by:

> How young art thou in this old age of time!
> How green in this gray world? Canst thou discern
> The signs of seasons, yet perceive no hint
> Or change in that stage-scene in which thou art
> Not a spectator but an actor? or
> Art thou a puppet moved by [enginery]? [10]

The sense that everywhere you look in the world you are victimized by your own illusions as well as the illusions of others is characteristic of Shelley's late poems; but this particular speech bears the marked imprint of Calderón's self-reflexiveness. One of Shelley's last translations from the Spanish playwright is a twenty-two line fragment from *La vida es sueño* that ends: 'All life and being are but dreams and dreams / Themselves are but the memory of other dreams.' [11] The citizens of this metropolis, as a stage world, are, of course, 'puppets moved by [enginery]'; only if we accept the stage illusion and peer into its mirror, do we take them as real. And yet, Shelley seems to be saying with this nest of stages (like Chinese boxes) that reality is also manipulated by illusions, whether it is Charles's claim to a divine right, or the Puritan zealots' belief in their own election. All mirrors distort reality, if only through reversal, and there is nothing but mirrors, including and most especially the mirror of our own mind.

The world of multiple, piecemeal illusions, the prismatic and many-sided mirror, Shelley creates in the first scene of *Charles the First* is further complicated by his introduction of Archy, the King's fool, in the second scene. The usual criticism, that Shelley borrows too heavily from the fool in *King Lear*, misses the point of why he does so, the function Archy serves in the scheme, such as we have it, of this play. As Charles himself characterizes Archy, 'He mocks and mimics all he sees or hears'.[12] He is, in other words, the very embodiment of the underlying dramatic principle Shelley is unfolding: he is a mirror, reversing perspectives, disassembling illusions, perhaps creating others. He so angers the single-minded Archbishop Laud that he is sent from the room. Upon returning, he hears of the intention of the parliamentarians — Hampden, Pym, and Sir Harry Vane — to emigrate to America, and he irreverently intrudes:

> Where they think to found
> A commonwealth like Gonzalo's in the play,
> Gynaecocoenic and pantisocratic.[13]

For a fool Archy commands a surprising knowledge of Greek: 'Gynaecocoenic' means sharing women in common. He also commands a surprising knowledge of the theatre created in the image of, to image, Charles's father, that is to say, James the First, for whose court *The Tempest* was written. Archy also seems to have a witty prescience about the scheme of Southey, Wordsworth, and Coleridge to found a pantisocracy, with shared women, in rural Pennsylvania a quarter century before Shelley wrote this fragment. The sudden intrusion of this anachronistic satirical jibe should not distract us from the remarkable insertion of *The Tempest*, both for itself and its context, into this hall of mirrors that is the state chamber of Charles. In this exact chamber a generation before the present masque is performed Charles's father would have observed, as in a mirror, Shakespeare's paradigm of the uses and abuses of power, his marriage masque, his representations of soaring spirit and debased flesh, his magus Prospero who creates dramatic illusions to edify or educate or terrify his audience and who knows that it is all an 'insubstantial pageant' that will melt 'into thin air'. So, too, will melt Charles's actual kingdom, a 'baseless fabric' for all its hauling of 'cloud-capped towers', 'gorgeous palaces', and other pieces of mere machinery through the streets of impoverished and dispirited London.

We are accustomed by Victorian conceptions of Shelley, not to mention André Maurois' distillation of them, to see Shelley as Ariel. In *Charles the First* he follows Shakespeare's own example, we might say, and casts himself as Prospero, maker and breaker of illusions. But the self-referentiality of the play, at least as it is sustained through the two long first scenes from which I have been quoting, reflects more than authorial manipulation. As I have been representing these scenes, they may seem strikingly close to theatrical experiments of a century later, for instance, those of Luigi Pirandello; but if so, it is less the unseen hand behind puppets who have taken independent life, as in *Sei Personaggi in cerca d'autore*, than it is the observer of the fictions of power in *Enrico Quattro*. As several commentators have noted, Shelley is surprisingly sympathetic to the plight of Charles and Henrietta. They are both trying to sustain illusions that are no longer possible, because no longer shared. Charles hates the brutality on which he must rely, the fanaticism that engulfs his supporters and opponents alike. They believe, with unquestioning devotion to their own rectitude, in mere symbols, illusions; but he as king must reconcile illusion and reality, or perhaps create the illusion of his solitary power from fatally contradictory fictions held by others. What is most characteristic of Shelley's protagonist in this fragment is that he *must* act and there is nothing he can do. He shares the dilemma of the Turkish sultan, Mahmud, in *Hellas*, of every member of the Cenci family, of Prometheus, and, interestingly enough, of Julian and Maddalo; also, if I may look slightly afield to our larger subject of inquiry, though there are signal differences, it is likewise the dilemma of Byron's Manfred, Marino Faliero, Jacopo Foscari, and the emperor Sardanapalus. Shelley did not get far enough into *Charles the First* for us to see how he would have shaped the problem — and, of course, he had to contend with the fact that history had already shaped it — but we can begin to discern in his portrait of Charles the outline of a consciousness trapped by illusions it can see through to an emptiness beyond, but which are necessary to its very existence.

In that impasse, if I may be forgiven a play on words that is very much to the point, passion lies. The power and potential significance of English Romantic drama — unfortunately, for the most part only potential and only explored long after the dramatists were dead — is in its focus not on action but on non-action: the frustration of purpose within irreconcilable claims or by multiple illusions none of which may be regarded as real. Before we concede too readily that this is the stuff of modern drama, we should realize how deeply embedded it was within the still-living inheritance of the early nineteenth-century European stage. Think for a minute of a dramaturgy that thrives on frustration and you will begin to cite the *Phèdre* or *Andromaque* of Racine, Otway's *Venice Preserved*, which exerted a strong authority for Byron and in which Eliza O'Neill had her greatest Drury Lane triumph, or, much closer to home — I mean Shelley's Pisan domicile as well as the period in which he lived — the tragedies of Vittorio Alfieri, which were translated into English by the early friend of Wordsworth and Coleridge, Charles Lloyd, in 1815. Byron was overwhelmed by the production of Alfieri's *Mirra* he saw in Bologna in August, 1819, and Shelley cited the same play as precedent for the subject of *The Cenci* in an 1820 letter to Hunt. We tend to think of neoclassical drama as cold, static, full of speech; and it is true that in his *Defence of Poetry* Shelley generally condemns the frigid productions of the English Restoration. But the conventions and structural principles of neoclassical tragedy, and especially its emphasis on the expression of passion, were still very much current in the European Romantic theatre.

If we recall the exchange of letters between Shelley and Byron on the models for the dramaturgy of *The Cenci* and *Marino Faliero*, what we will find of most relevance is not that Shelley championed Jacobean and Byron neoclassical tragedy, but that neoclassical drama is the closer in time and still a living tradition to play against. The putative jacobeanism of *The Cenci* seems to me a wholly false issue, though it has again been raised by reviewers of the 1985 production of Shelley's tragedy done by the Bristol Old-Vic Company: the adapter of two of the seven extant plays of Aeschylus, the recreator of Aristophanes, and translator of Euripides, not to mention the Homeric hymns and Plato, is certainly a neo-Hellenist if not strictly a neoclassicist. When Shelley remarks, both in the preface to *The Cenci* and in the *Defence*, that great drama rises by virtue of its poetry to an ideal and universal contemplation, he is endorsing a neoclassical dramatic aesthetic. The long speeches of all Romantic drama are the most obvious example of that aesthetic, and when they are regularly condemned by British and American critics as suggesting that the authors were only poets and could not bring themselves to write for the stage, such critics only confess their ignorance of the conditions and expectations of that contemporary stage, and, worse, of the true history of European drama. As with the

Victorians' distortions of Shelley, that history of drama is in danger of being reduced to footnotes or to the storage vaults of museums: quaint, antiquated, the symptom of an unenlightened and undramatic age. Not to indulge in a long speech of my own, let me simply observe that the great age of the London theatre, from Garrick to Kean, treated such speeches as we do arias in opera. The star system thrived on them, the audiences cheered them, and a few great poets, among whom we number Byron and Shelley, wrote them.

Such speeches are not inherently undramatic, but they do represent a kind of drama from which we are increasingly distant, one that depends on rhetoric for the expression of emotion and whose central concern is the sensibility of a character. What is most remarkable about *The Cenci* is not its borrowings from this author or that, or its attempts to represent monstrous evil or crushed saintliness on stage, but that we as an audience should be asked to concern ourselves so intimately with the state of mind of Beatrice in its minute adjustments to harrowing circumstance. But the same is true of Phèdre and especially true of Racine's *Andromaque* where every principal figure, except the title character who is the still point at the centre, is at one moment or another truly crazy. It is a dramaturgy not of action but of psychology, not of doing but of being, and in that exemplary work of a being that defies ultimate analysis. And Shelley brings to such a tradition, whose origins he would have traced directly from Calderón de la Barca, a refined sense of its values, as we have seen with the prisms within prisms of *Charles the First*. Or, to cite the clear parallel in *Prometheus Unbound*, the eyes of Panthea into which Asia peers to discern the essence of Prometheus: 'dark, far, measureless, — / Orb within orb, and line through line inwoven'.[14]

The 'orb within orb' can suggest the nuanced complexity of truth or the progressive stripping away of illusion, or perhaps both at the same time. It can lead an Asia to the depths of consciousness where she confronts the power of will that is Demogorgon and effects a liberation. It can lead a Beatrice Cenci to the increasing awareness that every element on which she has built her ethics is an illusion and thus to the brink of the abyss on which Giacomo Leopardi would stand within a decade. Shelley's drama is a drama of character, but of character grappling with thought. Though it is subtly political in implication, it is not so much ideological as profoundly concerned with the underlying power of ideas on the mind. The point at which this fundamental attribute of Shelleyan drama becomes clearest is in the middle of *Hellas*, when, with reports of battles being won and lost — the traditional stuff of drama — flourishing about the stage, the ancient Wandering Jew, Ahasuerus, convinces the sultan Mahmud that they scarcely matter:

> Thought
> Alone, and its quick elements, Will, Passion,
> Reason, Imagination, cannot die;
> They are, what that which they regard, appears,
> The stuff whence mutability can weave
> All that it hath dominion o'er, worlds, worms,
> Empires and superstitions — what has thought
> To do with time or place or circumstance? [15]

What, one might ask, is a statement like this doing at the centre of a drama whose purpose is ostensibly propaganda — Romantic agitprop — for a nationalist revolution? And the answer could be very complex indeed. For *Hellas* is a drama, and Ahasuerus is a character among several within it.[16] His conversation with the dispirited Mahmud wholly disarms the sultan, Shelley's point perhaps being that tyranny is unnatural and inherently self-destructive. But Mahmud is disarmed metaphorically, mentally. Even as his soldeirs win the battle for him, he has lost his will to win it, and the ultimate triumph of the Greeks is implied. So that Ahasuerus represents the truth of this drama, that ideas constitute the premises for action, that mental liberation is a condition for political liberation, that an ancien regime, as Shelley expresses it in his preface, can try to repress, but cannot long survive, a change in consciousness.

Yet Ahasuerus is not alone in representing such a formidably idealist version of reality: rather he virtually repeats the formulation of Asia as she asks of Demogorgon, 'Who made all [this world] contains — thought, passion, reason, will, / Imagination?' [17] Not flowers, not animals, not even cities, nor indeed citizens, but thought — thought and its mental constituents. *Hellas*, like *Charles the First*, is deeply concerned with how minds structure — or how they stage — reality. Mahmud, in summoning the shade of his ancestor Mahomet the Second, suggests that the living are dead, he most especially, and the chorus reminds us that the dead are alive:

> Greece and her foundations are
> Built below the tide of war,
> Based on the chrystalline sea
> Of thought and its eternity;
> Her citizens, imperial spirits,
> Rule the present from the past,
> On all this world of men inherits
> Their seal is set.[18]

The Cenci has been purposefully left to the side in this discussion in order to gather the materials for a framework for its understanding. I do not think that the proper framework is moral — does Beatrice's murder of her father reveal her corruption? — though I would remark that the 'restless and anatomizing casuistry' with which critics continue to argue over that problem is a splendid vindication of Shelley's intellectual purpose in writing the tragedy. But he states clearly in the preface that the drama has no simple moral purpose; then he focuses on the intrinsic idea that motivates it, which is an involved and wholly involving symbol-system, that of the church, which touches all aspects of life, and can be constrained to evil purposes as to good. There is a sense in which the properties of that symbol-system are as much carried across the stage set here as are the fragments of the state mythology at the beginning of *Charles the First*. The process is more internalized, and it is centred in the consciousness of Beatrice Cenci, who first sees herself trapped by a family tyranny and sexual politics, then enlarges her focus to recognize that these are supported by a state system, then comes to see that the state system is itself dependent upon mystified religious symbols on which she herself depends, in which she herself believes. The enduring power of *The Cenci* stems from its steadfast recognition that human beings are raped metaphysically when they place their absolute faith in conceptions that are only metaphorical. The last veil stripped away before Beatrice's unblinking eye is that of universal justice as something beyond human control. I am not, I trust, mitigating the physical violence suffered in this drama, but finally it is that misplaced sense of justice, the creation of a male power structure that relies on its absoluteness to perpetuate its tyrannies, that is responsible for Beatrice's being ravished and for its mental consequences. She is raped by the idea of God lodged within her father's person. By the end of the drama she is no longer self-victimized, but, insofar as her entire society *is* self-victimized, she is wholly isolated. There is nothing to be liberated into except the execution chamber.

The dramatic universe I have been describing must, in its sum, seem at least curious, perhaps quite odd. The form that is by its mode most objective is forced to become the vehicle for the subjective. Action is curtailed and thought magnified. In the extreme case, *Prometheus Unbound*, a simple change of heart alters the universe. And then the spectacle is continually observed observing itself: in holding up a mirror to the audience, it catches itself in the reflection of holding up a mirror to the audience. And so it goes, on and on, reflection after reflection, like the course of thought, the stream of universal consciousness, itself. Odd, yes; but fascinating, too. And certainly not unique by modern standards: Samuel Beckett has built a major theatrical career out of these materials. But of course, there is a difference, and it is crucial. For Shelley did possess a unitary faith within his sceptical philosophical idealism. To recognize that thought and its conceptions are primary, for him, is immediately to acknowledge that society is dependent upon, conditioned by, them. His dramas are records of mental liberation, by which ideas imply social action, essences are caught in the process of embodying themselves in human form. The prism that contemplates its own stage machinery is not simply suggesting that all art is a game. On the contrary, it is suggesting that we bring multi-faceted symbols into life in order to see through them and into ourselves, not to mystify them into an objective status. The drama that can liberate by representing the processes of thought and the essence of human character can also become the mask for codified tyranny.

Byron's drama suggests the same dangers, though, curiously for one who created himself in his narrative poetry as the archetypal hero, in his drama Byron is never as self-reflexive as Shelley. Byronic theatre is more focused on the conflict between individual self-assertion and the inertial pressures of culture, class, religion, history itself. But Shelley appears to have conceived of drama as a theoretical abstraction, and I mean nothing pejorative in putting it that way. As we might expect from Shelley's penetrating and highly literary mind, what is ultimately most important to him are the implications of the dramatic mode itself. Drama objectifies, yet necessarily calls attention to the fictions by which it creates its supposed objectivity. Not only its fictions but its very temporality belie that objectivity, if we think, as we tend to, of the objective as static. My sense is that what drew Shelley to drama was the very idea of motion, because drama is the literary form whose very essence is in motion. It creates objectivities but not fixities. Drama, in this conception, is like the process of thought itself, which is, as Ahasuerus asserts, the only constant there is, but whose constancy is an absolute paradox, apparent in its never stopping, being always in movement. Aristotle claims that objective representation is the mimesis of action. But the real action for Shelley is in the mind. And it is that action, the incessant process of thought, that Shelley's drama attempts to imitate, to mirror, and to encourage. The self-reflexiveness of Shelleyan drama is the opposite of playful; it is watchful, cautionary. Beware of being trapped by your own symbols, he says, like all those poor captives chained to Life's chariot in *The Triumph of Life*. Beware of converting fictions into fixities. Beware — and be free.

FOUR:
ROMANTIC DRAMA IN PERFORMANCE

Richard Allen Cave

The patent puppet-shows of this mighty metropolis are swayed and supplied by individuals who have no emulation but in the race of gain; rash, ignorant, and rapacious, they have rendered the stage a medium of senseless amusement, and if their sordid earnings could be secured by a parricidal sacrifice of the drama itself, we do not scruple to confess our belief that such a detestable sacrifice would be readily effected. If Mr. Shelley has ever speculated in the remotest manner upon an appeal to the stage, we urge him, most earnestly, to renounce that intention.[1]

So Shelley was advised — surprisingly by no less a journal than the *Theatrical Inquisitor* in April 1820 — on the publication of *The Cenci*. Shelley certainly had ambitions to see the play performed: he informed Peacock that he had 'taken some pains to make my play fit for representation';[2] moreover being nothing if not ambitious he already had in mind a preferred cast — Eliza O'Neill for Beatrice and Kean for the Count. The Lord Chamberlain's ban because of the play's concern with incest kept *The Cenci* off the stage till 1886 and even then it had to be performed privately. The advice was sound: the play was too good for the contemporary stage, if one is to judge by the fate that overtook one of Byron's dramas that was produced. On completing *Manfred* Byron wrote to Hobhouse: 'I have at least rendered it *quite impossible* for the stage'.[3] He later added a sadly prophetic rider: it is, he observed, 'a sort of mad Drama,' written 'for the sake of introducing the Alpine scenery in description'.[4] That last phrase might also be read as a direct challenge. Drury Lane failed to rise to the bait; Covent Garden, however, did in the form of Mr. Alfred Bunn in 1834, who, noting the growing vogue for John Martin's spectacular canvases,[5] mounted a version of the play which J. Westland Marston considered was perpetrated 'less for its own sake than for that of its gorgeous spectacular frame'.[6] Henry Crabb Robinson who saw a performance confided to his Diary that he 'sat through *Manfred* without any pleasure whatever except from the splendid scenery'.[7] This was not the last time that Byron's artistry was elbowed to one side by an ambitious manager wishing to highlight the skills of his stage designer.

Marston who saw the play in his youth was nonetheless sufficiently impressed by it that he could in later age remember some details of the acting with pleasure as matching Byron's conception:

> Miss Ellen Tree (whom I then saw for the first time) declaimed the lines allotted to the Witch of the Alps — lines which are not only few, but almost devoid of dramatic force, serving only to draw out Manfred's long and gloomy retrospect. Nevertheless, in her appearance, as she stood within the arch of a rainbow — in her garments, which seemed woven of aerial colours touched by the sun — and in her voice, the tones of which, though sweet, were remote and passionless — she realized all the weird charm of a genius of lake and mountain. There was something glacial in her unsubstantial loveliness, something that belonged to the forms of sleep rather than those of common day.[8]

Equally memorable was the Manfred of Mr. Denvil:

> Boy though I was when I saw him in this part, I still remember his pale, almost spectral face, thrown out by his dark garb, and a haughty isolation and melancholy in tone, look and gesture that well conveyed the mingled pride and remorse of one who, though racked by the sense of a hidden crime, has won commerce with supernatural beings.[9]

More germane to my immediate purpose, however, is Marston's recollection that a few nights later he was taken to the Strand Theatre to see *Man-Fred*, 'a capital burlesque', in which a comedian named Mitchell performed the principal character:

> When the curtain rose, and Mitchell — I think, as a working bricklayer — inspected with gloomy dejection an empty quart measure, there was in his first utterance —
> 'The jug must be replenished; but even then
> It will not hold so much as I could drink;'
> a deep, fixed, self-absorbed despondency, which recalled, with delightful absurdity, Denvil's tones as Lord Byron's hero —
> 'The lamp must be replenished; but even then
> It will not burn so long as I must watch'.[10]

Despite one's amusement at this, one cannot but sympathise with Byron's hatred of the 'insolence of the Green Room' and understand his dismissal of actors as a species of 'strutters and fretters'.

If one chose to define the quality of prevailing theatrical taste it would have to be — with a few notable exceptions — popularist and consequently indifferent towards attempts to create new forms of verse tragedy. Some facts will amplify my critical point. The same year (1813) that saw Coleridge's *Remorse* staged at Drury Lane (itself a relative success) witnessed the first performance of Isaac Pocock's *The Miller and his Men*, a sensational melodrama that held a place in the popular repertoire of the major, minor and provincial houses until the 1870s. While only seven performances of Byron's *Marino Faliero* were given at Drury Lane in 1821, Moncrieff's *Tom and Jerry*, a farce based on Pierce Egan's *Life in London*, was such a success at the Adelphi that same season that six imitations of it were presented at rival establishments within the next three years. Though Macready's personal fondness for Byron's *Werner* was to keep the play continually in revival after its first production in 1830, he was never to equal the number of performances in the role that T. P. Cooke achieved in the part of William in Jerrold's nautical melodrama, *Black-Eyed Susan*, that entailed the actor's dancing a celebrated double hornpipe. A fact equally relevant to my argument here is that the most popular of Byron's works in the theatre in the nineteenth century was not even written in the dramatic form: *Mazeppa*, dramatised by H. M. Milner, was first staged at Astley's Amphitheatre in 1831 and underwent numerous revivals, most notably with Adah Isaacs Menken playing the title role *en travestie*. Posters depicting her strapped to a horse naked — she in fact wore exceptionally tight fleshings — lured audiences back to Astley's in 1864 when other spectacles in the play had long since ceased to excite. An age of melodrama, burlesque, equestrian spectaculars did not look kindly on dramatists whose values were other and centred on the presentation of subtle psychological nuance and on preserving the integrity of the tragic tradition. Friction and disdain colour the relations between the contemporary stage and most of the Romantic poets. In the closing moments of Byron's tragedy *Sardanapulus*, his hero leaps into a funeral pyre claiming his act is 'a light / To lesson ages'.[11] Anne Barton in a brilliant study of the poet's plays [12] has argued that here Byron is expressing his belief that history rightly understood can enlighten future generations and that, anticipating Brecht in many ways, Byron saw historical tragedy as an intellectual rather more than an emotional exercise of the imagination. Could Sardanapalus's great cry not also be seen to express the hope that future forms of theatre and theatrical practice might be more sympathetic towards Byron's intentions than contemporary conditions were? Byron knew things could be different, more importantly knew that they *had been* different: there were the past examples of Shakespeare and Aeschylus (Shelley would doubtless add Calderón to the list); and there was the contemporary example of Alfieri (a fortnight after suffering convulsions during the performance,[13] he confided to Murray: 'I have never been quite well since the night of the representation of Alfieri's *Mirra*').[14] With Alfieri's work he felt in the presence of a kindred spirit, a potential realised; mention of the Italian dramatist in his correspondence invariably accompanies a sarcastic thrust at the expense of the English theatre. Yet even there during his own lifetime things had been different; always excepting Kean, there had been a change for the worse. Eliza O'Neill he refused to see, lest she disturbed his recollections of Mrs. Siddons; he admired Cooke, Kemble and Kean but considered 'Mrs. Siddons worth them all put together'.[15] Medwin remarks in his *Conversations of Lord Byron* that nothing equalled Kemble's Coriolanus in the poet's estimation and avers that if Kemble 'had acted "Marino Faliero", its fate would have been very different'.[16] Clearly for Byron a certain sense of style, of tragic decorum had gone, a stateliness of bearing and of utterance that was powerful by virtue of its technique of deliberate understatement that allowed the dramatist's language to capture an audience's imagination. Byron could be fatalistic; but often like Yeats, another poet for whom the contemporary time was out of joint, he could give his assent to a philosophy of cyclic change and renewal. Times were to change for Byron and shortly — though Macready lacked much of Kemble's poise and grandeur; and they are changing still. Changes in theatrical practice this century are making for a situation increasingly conducive to a proper appreciation of the Romantic poets' theatrical sensitivity. There is today a far less prescribed definition of what constitutes 'good' theatre. But this is to anticipate my argument. We must first explore the annals of stage history and trace the fortunes of Romantic drama in performance.

* * * * *

Wordsworth's *The Borderers*, composed in 1795-6, printed in 1842, was not played till the year of the bi-centenary of his birth, 1970, and then by a group of amateurs, the Grasmere Players. Their mode of performance intimated an unease with the play since they chose to set it in a frame of their own devising: some villagers of Grasmere in 1820 were shown as offering the play to Wordsworth as a birthday treat. The effect was to distance the audience from the play as a literary curiosity by stressing the amateurishness of the company's effort. The performance in fact had considerable polish, especially in the sensitive handling of the verse, which came across not as learned speeches (always a danger with amateurs) but as the expression of thinking and feeling individuals. Far from being the fustian some adverse critics have claimed, the verse had considerable drive. The excellence of the speaking, however, drew attention to a deficiency in the chosen style of verse as a dramatic medium of expression: it continually describes rather than defines or, better still, renders character. All the characters in the main plot speak with, as it were, one voice, share the same style of verse. Oswald, an Iago-like deceiver, is attempting to poison Marmaduke's mind so that, murdering Lord Herbert, he will come to share Oswald's fallen condition of obsessive guilt. Duplicity is the essence of Oswald's nature, yet when he talks to us in soliloquy out of a private self about his evil intentions, the verse conveys the same tone and is couched in the same confident aphoristic expression that is elsewhere used when he talks about honour and integrity with Marmaduke while seeking deviously to seduce him to criminal ways. There is no dramatic realisation of Oswald's two selves so that his attempts to pervert Marmaduke lack the horror and fascination of Iago's undermining of Othello's sanity.

The most 'living' characters — as one might expect of Wordsworth — proved in performance to be the peasants like Eldred and Eleanor who succour the afflicted heroine and her father, and the beggar woman whom Oswald suborns to aid his schemes. The vitality of these creations made one regret that Wordsworth had not developed as combative and revolutionary an approach to drama as to lyrical poetry to make peasant experience the whole subject of a play written like the *Lyrical Ballads* in 'a selection of language really used by men'.[17] This is not quite the idle speculation it might at first seem: the 1790s saw a growing popular taste for melodrama of a rural and domestic nature (Thomas Holcroft wrote the most notable examples of the type); Wordsworth could have taken the conventions and idiom of such plays and with his depth of insight into the realities of the life of the country poor might have transformed that style of drama into something richer because truer to social fact.

That this is not an idle speculation is given further weight by the example of Coleridge, who was the only romantic poet-dramatist to know theatrical success in his own lifetime. *Remorse*, written under the title of *Osorio* contemporaneously with *The Borderers*, though rejected by Sheridan and Kemble in 1797, was staged at Drury Lane on 23 January 1813. It was given twenty performances; Coleridge was lionised for a while and met with a little prosperity: 'It has been a good thing for the Theatre. They will get 8 or 10,000£ — & I shall get more than all my literary Labours put together . . . 400£: including the Copy-right'.[18] That *Remorse* was a success is not surprising: Coleridge's finest poems — *The Rime of the Ancient Mariner, Christabel, Kubla Khan* — show him taking currently popular material, Gothick mystery or literary Orientalism, as vehicles to explore his own unique sensibility, enabling his readers to pass beyond the familiar into territories of experience that are strange but imaginatively compelling. *Remorse* has superficially all the trappings of Gothick melodrama: an exotic historical location (Spain at the time of Philip II's persecution of the Moors); supernatural dealings; sorcery; two murders in eerie settings (a moonlit cave with torrent and chasm and a grim dungeon). But these trappings are not ends in themselves; rather they help to define the mind of the central character, Ordonio, a younger brother obsessed with jealousy of his senior, Alvar, whom he believes for much of the play he has successfully murdered. But jealousy wars for supremacy in his mind with more natural feelings of affection. The conventions of Gothick melodrama are deployed by Coleridge to give insight into the strange workings of the human psyche, as is made clear in a letter he wrote to Southey defending the play against Gifford's criticism: his subject, he claims, is not sensational event but the 'Anguish and Disquietude arising from the Self-contradiction introduced into the Soul by Guilt — a feeling which is good or bad according as the Will makes use of it . . . & Remorse is every where distinguished from virtuous Penitence'.[19] *Remorse* investigates moral and psychological discriminations of a peculiarly Coleridgean kind. That this was not a subjective interpretation of the play but one that was readily communicated during the performance to an attentive spectator is shown by the review carried by the *Morning Chronicle* two days after the first night: the critic welcomed the play as a rare theatrical experience because of Coleridge's concern with 'what may be called the underplot of the character' of Ordonio; 'there is scarcely any other dramatic writer who has so much as attempted to describe the involuntary, habitual reaction of the passions and understanding on each other'.[20]

More crucial to my discussion of the reasons for the success of *Remorse* is the amount of evidence that shows Coleridge *cared* for the fate of his play in the theatre. He attended Drury Lane and noted audience responses — as any good dramatist must — especially those reactions that showed his artistry had achieved his particular intentions. The poet emerges as a surprisingly good judge of acting:

Poor Rae [the actor who played Ordonio] . . . did the best in his power — & is a good man . . . a moral, & affectionate Husband & Father — But Nature has denied him Person, & all volume & depth of Voice; so that the blundering Coxcomb, Elliston [as Alvar], by mere dint of Voice & Self-conceit out-dazzled him.[21]

Yet the play had the power to transcend such apparent disadvantages, particularly at the climax, which pleased Coleridge for conveying more than merely the event: Alvar's revelation of his identity was less the focus of attention than the complex reverberations this produced in the depths of Ordonio's psyche:

Spite of wretched Acting the Passage told wonderfully, in which as a struggle between two unequal . . . Wrestlers, the weaker had for a moment got uppermost — & Ordonio, with unfeigned Love & genuine repentence, says — I will kneel to thee my Brother! Forgive me, Alvar! — till the Pride, like the Bottom-swell on our Lake, *gusts* up again in — *Curse* me with forgiveness.[22]

Coleridge sensed a further, subtler strength in the play which poor acting did not mar:

> The second Good quality is, I think, the variety of metres, according as the Speeches are merely transitive; or narrative; or passionate; or (as in the Incantation) deliberate & formal Poetry. It is true, they are all or most Iambic Blank Verse; but under that form there are 5 or 6 perfectly distinct metres.[23]

Unlike Wordsworth, Coleridge was clearly conscious, as these comments show, of the need to characterise *through* the verse and perceptive of the ways in which variety of poetic metres could affect variety of mood and of dramatic pace in performance. Fine sentiments and moral discriminations are not enough to sustain a play in the theatre. None of the other Romantic poet-dramatists, not even Byron with his working knowledge of Drury Lane, was as fascinated as Coleridge, given his analytical mind, with the *process* of theatre in performance; only Coleridge as a consequence could gauge how his art succeeded in despite of the limitations of the performers. Byron was much impressed with *Remorse*, hoped for a revival of the play with Kean as Ordonio, and urged Coleridge to write more plays for Drury Lane once he was on the subcommittee of management; but nothing came of it all. Southey was of the opinion that had *Remorse* not been rejected initially in 1797 but had succeeded then when Coleridge was a younger and less afflicted man, he might have proved himself capable of completing a fine new play every season.[24] This is shrewd criticism: *Remorse* has its weaknesses but continuing experience of the practice of theatre by a mind as acutely perceptive as Coleridge's would have eliminated the like from future efforts.

* * * * *

It is tempting to speculate how Shelley would have reacted to the realities of the contemporary stage if *The Cenci* had reached production during his lifetime. Would it have transformed his poetic style completely as happened with that erstwhile Shelleyan, W. B. Yeats, when he became embroiled in theatre business at the Abbey? Perhaps it is as well it were not acted, given the hysteria at the time of its publication: 'It seemed to be the production of a fiend and calculated for the entertainment of devils in hell'.[25] What a study of Shelley's Preface shows is that he worked with a serious attention to what with regard to Coleridge was termed the 'underplot of character'. He carefully analyses his dramatic technique as deployed in the scene for Cenci and Lucretia, his wife, that preceds his murder (IV.i.), defining the complexity of motive in both characters at this point in the action. Yet to study the scene itself is to realise how little of this motivation is *stated*, as would be the case in contemporary melodrama.[26] This is drama that poses a challenge to the actors to make clear the moral and psychological patterning which is subtly implicit in the writing. Given the sustained intensity of tone in the verse (Shelley's characters seem to *think* at their very nerve ends), it is tempting for an actor to go for histrionic display, to see the text as melodrama and play on the surface thereby failing to *inhabit* the text in its full richness, as Shelley clearly intended him to do. Shelley, I would argue, leaves room for an actor's powers of interpretation to realise the full potentialities of a role: he has freedom to explore the relation between statement and subtext. These points can be developed and substantiated by a study of the stage history of the play, which has received four notable British productions: a private showing by the Shelley Society at the Grand Theatre, Islington, in May, 1886; a revival with Sybil Thorndike, directed by Lewis Casson at the New Theatre, 1920-21; a staging at the Old Vic by Michael Benthall in April, 1959; and a recent revival by the Bristol Old Vic Studio in 1985. The frequency of the play's revival compared with the fate of other Romantic drama itself attests to the stage-worthiness of *The Cenci* and its attraction to good actors.

A glance at the records shows the variety of possibilities in interpreting Count Cenci. Hermann Vezin in 1886, doubtless perturbed by the play's reputation, trusted to the proven excellence of his elocutionary skills to keep the full horrors of the part at a distance, to the evident relief of the reviewer for *The Times*.[27] This was perhaps a more sensible approach than it might at first appear: it saved the production from being merely a *succès de scandale*; more importantly the effect could be to engage the audience's attention on Shelley's argument that what drives Beatrice inexorably to atheism is the discovery that her father's tyranny is reduplicated in the State, the Church and the processes of the Law, that she battles to win herself a freedom that is everywhere denied her as a human right. Judging from the *Times* review, which complains of the tedium of a four-hour long performance, this larger possibility of interpretation was not realised; given the short rehearsal-time devoted to productions of this kind, it is hardly surprising that the cast failed to find adequately the play's inner life and dynamic.

Robert Farquharson in 1920 took a wholly different line as might be supposed of one who had achieved a certain notoriety as Herod in Wilde's *Salomé*; he positively over-reached himself in attempting a second portrait of decadent senility. To judge by Agate's review, Farquharson worked too long and too hard at the depravity of the role:

> The actor over-mouthed his words, pulling his jowl as though he would put the whole of hell into each single phrase. Being overdone, the evil was less than implacable; you felt that it was painted on the cheek, not that it came from the soul. These, you whispered your neighbour, were the faces that Quilp made to intimidate his spouse. The voice, too, was light in quality and before the final curse was reached conviction was spent. Nevertheless, the performance was obviously informed with intelligence, but to claim for it the highest degree of tragic, or even horrific, passion is to forget Irving.[28]

The comparison with Irving is telling, Irving being a master at projecting subtle portraits of the psychology of evil. Clearly Farquharson went for the surface and not the subtext; indeed his dated melodramatic exhibitionism argues a basic unease with the power of Shelley's language to convey such subtlety as Agate patently felt was present in the writing and conception of the role and might be depicted with precision, given a different style of performance.

Hugh Griffith who essayed the role in 1959 is a Welsh actor with a fine ringing tone and largeness of stature and of stage personality who is yet capable of surprisingly witty understatement (Falstaff and Brecht's Azdak are numbered among his particular successes). He brought to the part a degree of 'humanising restraint' [29] by relishing the possibilities for insinuation; his Cenci was a depraved being who was the more frightening in that, in his own eyes and evaluation, he was a suave and worldly gentleman. He was a monster because he found a source of humour in his own evil conceptions and so was beyond guilt or remorse: to borrow Hamlet's phrase, he was a damned because a smiling villain. This saved the performance from toppling into melodramatic excess or absurdity.

William Hoyland for Bristol Old Vic started from a wholly different premise with the role in choosing to play him as a relatively youthful character, as a being who insidiously thrived on his cruelty. This gave his performance an evil charisma and a quiet intensity that created a great sense of danger when he was on stage (Hoyland had recently played Dionysus in *The Bacchae* of Euripides where this same total self-command matched with a predatory power were deployed to excellent effect).[30] Hoyland stressed the complete Renaissance patrician in Cenci as a matter not simply of bearing but of an awareness of his *absolute* authority over others. He despised his numerous victims and the lackeys who waited in attendance at his banquet because they had become utterly subservient to his will. Beatrice was a different case: her spirited appeal for help against his tyranny from the nobles and fathers of Rome patently excited him, for here was a new challenge to his power: a will as strong as his own to break asunder, a pristine consciousness to suffuse with horror and despair. It was a harrowing portrayal for being so glacial and so elegant in gesture, movement, turn of speech. A brute inexorable force lurked behind a mesmeric animal grace. The production inserted several short mimed scenes, Expressionist in style, to clarify the development of the plot (Shelley is curiously coy about the theme of incest and it is not exactly clear for the uninitiated what Cenci's nameless crime against his daughter is); one such occurred between Acts I and II. In an eerie light, Cenci appeared behind Beatrice; bending, seemingly to kiss her neck, he savagely gripped her hair then sinuously unfastened it, tore off the sleeve of her dress, then delicately uncoiled her belt, and suddenly disappeared leaving the girl a prey to uncertainty and terror. Not only did this moment epitomise Hoyland's whole approach to the role as a man to whom money and social status give a complete moral freedom, it also gave the Beatrice a firm psychological ground from which to convey believably and with considerable pathos the growing hysteria that overtakes her character in the central acts. The inter-relation between this Cenci and his daughter was throughout tense with meticulously observed psychological nuances that encouraged one to relish Shelley's command of characterisation as the force creating the inner structure and momentum of the play.

How to structure the character of Beatrice is a real test of an actress's sensitivity; crucially, how to motivate the last act. Interestingly this is where there seems over the various productions to have been the widest variety of interpretation. From the first readers seem almost wilfully to have missed Shelley's point that the refusal of Beatrice's world to understand her struggle to define an integrity of mind drives her relentlessly to atheism as a last refuge of her sanity:

> You do well telling me to trust in God.
> I hope I do trust in Him. In whom else
> Can any trust? And yet my heart is cold.[31]

It is a rare test for an actress to accomplish this shift from a victim to a visionary who finds in crime a clarity of insight into more equitable ways of ordering society, thus rendering herself vulnerable to a Church and State anxious to protect their privileges. Henry Crabb Robinson missed the grandeur of Shelley's conception completely: of Beatrice in the final scenes he observed in his *Diary* (March 23, 1845):

At first I objected to her wilful denial of the truth, but her motive is the allowable infirmity of noble minds. To save the family honour she lied to the last.[32]

Noble Beatrice is, but not on such mundane grounds; it lies rather in her strength of mind that can transcend the horror of discovering that beyond the battle with Cenci lies a greater battle with a paternalistic Deity, that tyranny is the true nature of a principle in the universe to which till now she has given unquestioning assent.

Alma Murray, the first Beatrice in 1886, was generally praised for the way 'she husbanded her much-taxed resources',[33] and did so by exercising a scrupulous intelligence. That that intelligence baulked at the implications of Shelley's conclusion is evident from the *Times* review of her performance:

Beatrice's character is necessarily in some degree sympathetic; but the poet commits a strange mistake in view of the dramatic exigencies of the case in making her, after her own dishonour and her father's murder, cling with such tenacity to life as to forswear herself in the judge's presence. Her sudden change of front is incomprehensible. Never a ray of hope is allowed to penetrate the mass of horrors so vividly depicted.[34]

To the Victorian sensibility, for Beatrice the fallen woman death was the only proper end — a death sought in patience and humility. No way could this reviewer's set of values encompass Shelley's depiction of Beatrice's visionary zeal and find in it a proper tragic decorum.

It was just this ecstatic moral awakening that Sybil Thorndike brought to the part at the close. Agate, who neither liked the play nor Sybil Thorndike (generally) as an actress, was nonetheless thrilled by her performance here:

Cenci dispatched, a new spirit at once disengaged itself. The motive changed from incest to parricide, and what I have called the second storey of spiritual significance became apparent in Miss Thorndike's idealized figure of Injury and in the justiciary's identification of her deed of murder with that of rebellion against the paternal authority of the Church. One felt that if Beatrice had been the chief figure in a non-metaphysical tragedy she would have trumpeted her guilt and proclaimed it innocence. Here she was, however, equivocating like a Greek and lying like a Trojan, fighting authority with its own weapons. Subtle as any casuist, and since to her this killing was no murder, she swore roundly that she had no hand in it. More than ever was Miss Thorndike the play here. First she had been an individual victim, then a symbol of maiden virtue rudely strumpeted, and now she rose to the embodiment of a pure philosophic idea — the idea of Rebellion. This was what Shelley, whose ruling passion was revolt, was after.[35]

Agate goes on to define the quintessential quality of Thorndike's acting style as a certain 'hardness': 'In plays like *The Cenci* this hardness has extraordinary value: it enables you to see through it to the play'.[36] Sarah Bernhardt, he opines, could not play the part; she would have an audience weeping copiously and one would see neither the stage nor the play for 'a mist of tears'. Thorndike, by contrast, never works for pathos; she achieves it by virtue of a moral grit that will not let her seek it overtly. Beatrice was as a consequence an ideal role for her because she could see it as a quest: Thorndike clearly was brilliant, resolute, enthralling in her attainment of a hard-won integrity in the final act; suffering and crime took her Beatrice to the threshold of a new world of perception and feeling. And such was Thorndike's controlled fervour that she carried her audience with her. This production of *The Cenci* was but a short step in time away from what was perhaps her finest characterisation: Shaw's Saint Joan (1924) — another being with an inner radiance who finds in herself the courage to throw off the shackles of Church and State to safeguard a private metaphysical awareness. As an actress she possessed an unrivalled ability to show how thought can in certain gifted individuals be an all-consuming passion. Her artistry was the perfect match for Shelley's conception.

Barbara Jefford (1959) attempted an intricate approach to the role: it seems from contemporary reviews [37] that she at once presented Shelley's evaluation of Beatrice and her own judgement of that stance as wayward. At this stage of her career Jefford was at her best in projecting a radiant honesty: in the Shakespeare 'Folio' seasons at the Old Vic earlier that decade she excelled as Viola and as Imogen; later she was herself to be a sturdily affectionate, no-nonsense Saint Joan. It seems as if she could only find a logic for Beatrice's actions within the constraints of her own stage personality by making her a study of a noble mind o'erthrown. This Beatrice did not so much grow in moral awareness as decline, losing all sense of scruple and discrimination, so overwhelming were the metaphysical repercussions of her involvement in the act of murder. She made a bid for freedom, but, rather like Macbeth, destroyed all pattern and meaning in the universe as a consequence. (This is one interesting way of handling the numerous 'echoes' of *Macbeth* throughout the text of *The Cenci*, making them an ironic commentary on the fate of the heroine.)[38] Jefford's speaking of the lies at the trial denying her involvement in the murder suggested a consciousness blindly struggling to save itself from annihilating despair as if Beatrice needed herself to believe the truth of what she was uttering. The lying was an act of desperate courage, a bid to save the self from total disintegration. *The Times* particularly praised Jefford's skill in distinguishing between courage here and mere effrontery. But having accepted this reading of the part, that reviewer realised Jefford had set herself 'the even more difficult task of showing that the collapse when the heroine faces execution comes about through a momentary failure of nerve and not through a sudden springing into activity of her imagination'.[39] The comment suggests that at this moment in the performance the text and the interpretation parted company. Beatrice's calm at the end with Lucretia and Bernardo sprang not, as with Thorndike, from inner assurance but was another effort of the will not to voice a fear of what might lie beyond the grave for a consciousness that has destroyed God. There was genuine pathos in the moment, but it was not the pathos Shelley devised. The *Times* critic liked the interpretation, but considered it difficult to accomplish because the actress received little help from Shelley; however, he did not go on to question whether it was therefore an accurate interpretation. This is an interesting case of an intelligent actress who saw the need to find an 'underplot of character' in performing *The Cenci* and who in large measure kept the emotional shape of the role as Shelley envisaged it, but by a subtle change of emphasis at the climax she contrived to make the experience of the play a much more comfortable and less challenging event for an audience than Thorndike's reading of the part. Jefford's Beatrice conformed to a conventional idea of tragic pathos — the murderer who became ironically the deed's creature — and missed the 'hardness' that Agate rightly detected as the core of Shelley's creation.

This was a weakness in Leonie Mellinger's recent portrayal at Bristol. She is a very young actress, gifted with a beautifully melodic voice and she capitalised on this in the early acts of the play to present very credibly the Beatrice who is the terrified victim of Cenci's torture; but she failed to make the transition to the mature Beatrice of the final scenes, who is much more than a plaintive girl lost in a malevolent world. Far from continuing to be the victim of circumstance, Beatrice takes on herself the shaping of destiny. But Leonie Mellinger played wholly for pathos (which is there certainly in the song to calm Lucretia and Giacomo and in the final business with the hair); she moved through the scenes without any attempt at interpretation, as if unaware of any change in Beatrice's psyche under the pressure of events. Mellinger and her director (Debbie Sherwell) seemed to baulk at the play's implications that guilt can shape the imagination for good and that the world, like her father, takes note of Beatrice only when her mind begins to aspire to vindicate her individuality and then takes note only to extinguish that mind with brutal promptitude. Unless an actress orchestrates this as a final movement in the relationship between Beatrice and her father, then the play lacks tension and momentum once Cenci himself is dead. The director certainly apprehended this pattern of connections since she cleverly had William Hoyland, who played Cenci, 'double' in the role of the judge at Beatrice's trial; but Leonie Mellinger failed to build on the possibilities this offered. This performance ended the play on a note of defeat, when the tone should, surely, be more intricate in its discriminations.

One cannot leave a discussion of *The Cenci* in performance without some reference to Artaud's version for his Theatre of Cruelty at the Folies-Wagram (May 6, 1935). One difficulty of Shelley's play for actors resides in the fact that they have in themselves to create the total atmosphere of the play and in a special sense: the richly imagistic verse throughout indicates the *quality* of each character's perceptions. The audience are, as it were, invited to enter into and share the atmosphere of the characters' minds as they are preyed upon by primal passions. Artaud cut the play to the bare bones of the text, replacing the imagistic content of the verse with surrealistic stage effects both visual and aural: at Cenci's banquet, for example, an orgiastic dimension was introduced by surrounding the actors with 'naked' dressmakers' dummies, while subdued bells and electronic sound waves are called for to keep time with the 'spinning rhythm' of the performers about the stage; the storm that accompanies the first attempt to murder the Count on his journey to Petrella is to be evoked by a howling wind against which the procession of characters in slow motion is seen to strain while disembodied voices intone Cenci's name relentlessly like great bursts of thunder; when Beatrice prepares the murderers for their second attempt on her father's life, she binds their voluminous cloaks around them till they resemble Egyptian mummies with only their fists exposed clutching the daggers, as if through a slow ritual she is extinguishing all their personality but the naked will to kill.[40] Far from imagining the characters' tortured perceptions, the audience are compelled by Artaud to share their disturbed modes of vision. In accordance with the doctrine behind the Theatre of Cruelty the play positively batters an audience's senses and sensibilities. Given that this is Artaud's primary objective, it is interesting to see how he handles the issue of Beatrice's development that we have been discussing. In the final scenes his cutting is most severe to highlight the sadism and hypocrisy of Beatrice's judges and accusers. Beatrice's own position is defined in one great cry of self-assertion when she turns on her tormentors who talk of payment for her sins: 'Pay for what? I am not guilty of the crime I committed'.[41] It is a brilliant conception and one sensitive to Shelley's purpose. Beatrice's mind recognises that her deed is a 'crime' by conventional standards of judgement but recognises too that Cenci's cruelty against her person and her soul so far outweigh the cruelty of her act in organising his murder that her consciousness is quite purged of responses like guilt and remorse. This is not a barefaced act of rebellion but an assertion of a new moral order that places the self rather than conventional morality as the arbiter of integrity. Artaud's Beatrice expects not to be understood by her judges who will impose on her the sentence of death, but her own sense of heightened moral scruple fearlessly urges her on. She refuses to placate them, preferring a searing anger. Artaud's version of the play is ultimately about the creating and refining of a new concept of conscience — a conscience that is answerable not to any social or religious code of values but to a rigorous and exacting sense of personal scruple. Artaud no more baulked at the full implications of the Shelley's tragedy than did Sybil Thorndike; he too recognised and accepted its essential 'hardness' and shaped out of Shelley's text a drama that anticipated much French existentialist theatre. For Artaud, Shelley was undeniably our contemporary.

* * * * *

Byron had early in his career made a name for himself in popular literature. Many critics, including Hazlitt and Lockhart, resented the fact that his dramas followed an elitist course and that Byron did not search for a theatrical equivalent to the 'fiery narrative-pace of *Lara*, or *The Giaour*'.[42] Byron knew the popular theatrical taste well of course from his year on the Drury Lane committee of management and he could, as his *Letters* abundantly show, advise would-be dramatists on how to revise work to achieve success in the popular vein (Maturin's melodrama, *Bertram*, being a notable example).[43] But by the time Byron turned to the drama as a form of personal expression, he had found Alfieri and it was in his 'simple and severe' style,[44] reminiscent for Byron of Aeschylus's work, that the poet found inspiration — a mode quite at variance with current English taste.

I wish to by-pass Elliston's notorious staging of *Marino Faliero* in April, 1821, as it has been well documented elsewhere, most fully by Marchand in his edition of the *Letters*.[45] Of more immediate relevance to my subject is Elliston's attempt later to persuade Byron to revise the play as a vehicle for Kean. Byron had championed Kean from his first appearances in London: to Kelly he vouchsafed the view, 'depend upon it this man is a man of genius' [46] and wrote later of Kean that 'he is the triumph of mind over matter for he has nothing but countenance and expression — his figure is very little & even mean — but I never saw the Passions so expressed — on the Stage at least — except by Mrs. Sid[don]s'.[47] When Elliston made his proposal, Byron, however, flatly refused. Interestingly Kean was not impressed by the idea either: James Winston's *Diaries* record the actor angrily telling Elliston that 'if it was the intention of playing the tragedy of Byron, the thought of having to study such trash would drive him from the country'.[48] Byron knew the scope of Kean's genius and knew it would not match his creation of Marino. Kean's greatest roles — Othello, Shylock, Richard III, Sir Giles Overreach — were all ones where passion is largely externalised, erupting into the action with a lethal dynamism. Byron's tragedies follow a different path: 'What I seek to show . . . is the *suppressed* passions — rather than the rant of the present day'.[49] The ideal actor for Byron's plays had to be found elsewhere. He appeared in the form of William Charles Macready. During his career he was to attempt productions of four of Byron's plays: *Werner* in 1830, which proved the most successful and was kept firmly by Macready in his repertoire till his retirement; *Sardanapalus* (1834); *The Two Foscari* (1838); and *Marino Faliero* (1842). To understand why Macready's technique and stage persona were ideal for conveying Byron's concern with suppressed passion we must turn to contemporary assessments of his style.

Westland Marston is one of the most carefully discriminating:

Of the qualities to which Macready owed his eminence, the highest and most remarkable were his psychological insight and his artistic power of translating his emotions into strikingly appropriate — often absolutely symbolic — forms of expression.[50]

He later amplified this point: 'The power of expressing states of feeling by gesture and attitude is, of course, necessary to every actor. With Macready it rose into a special endowment'.[51] Moreover Macready was, in Marston's view, gifted with a marvellous *ear*; his performances were always notable for 'his just perception of the right note of feeling even to a semi-tone'.[52] Marston gives numerous examples of Macready's virtuosity in these respects; two interesting cases relate to his performance in Byron's *Werner*.

First in discussing Macready's astonishing vocal transitions, he exemplifies the moment when Macready as the hunted and impoverished Werner meets again with his old enemy, Count Stralenheim, who is disturbed by the other man's watching presence but does not actually recognise him:

Nothing could be more curtly repellant than his [Macready's] tones, in answer to Stralenheim's questions —
Stral. Have you been here long?
Wer. (with abrupt surprise).   Long?
Stral.   I sought
    An answer, not an echo.
Wer. (rapidly and morosely). You may seek
    Both from the walls; I am not used to answer
    Those whom I know not.
A little later, when Stralenheim observes, 'Your language is above your station,' Werner's answer, '*Is it?*' contained a transition from ironical humility to scorn and loathing, which it was surprising so brief a phrase could express.[53]

Marston's instance of Macready's superlative powers as a mime is taken from a scene towards the end of the play. Count Stralenheim has been murdered in mysterious circumstances by Werner's son, Ulric, who has contrived to throw the appearance of guilt on another, a Hungarian named Gabor. Werner, as a consequence of his enemy's death, has become Count Siegendorf; he arrests and charges Gabor with the crime. Gabor in a long, calmly sustained narrative defends himself and tells the truth.

He [Gabor] is admitted, and answers Siegendorf's charge of murder by accusing Ulric of it, who is present. The Count, drawing, rushes on Gabor with fierce indignation, then turns from him with incredulous disdain. The latter, however, proceeds with his story. What Macready achieved here in the way of facial expression and symbolic gesture (for his share in the dialogue was small), has never, I think, under the given condition, been exceeded. At first, with one arm thrown fondly round his son's shoulder, he listened with light scorn to his accuser. As the proofs thickened, the eyes, before careless, became fixed on Gabor. This man related particular after particular, the fearful significance of which against his son the Count at length recognized, while the relaxed arm which lay on Ulric's shoulder fell heavily. As Gabor proceeded, and with increasing stress of proof, the Count turned and looked at his son. Shocked by his expression, he faltered a step from him. The tale continued, and again the stricken father unconsciously fell back. His changes of look and attitude had silently told all the effects of the story upon the sympathizing spectators.[54]

One can see instantly from this that excellent ensemble playing would be required of the actors if the double focus of this scene as recounted by Marston were to be achieved, the balance of interest between the speaking Gabor and the silent but deeply affected Werner. Macready valued sustained rehearsals with his fellow actors and one can see why; and also why he resented appearing with provincial companies in the role of star player when no concentrated and concerted preparation was allowed for.[55] Subtlety of effect was Macready's ambition: his *Journals* show him ever on guard against the easy excuse for rant; and show him fascinated by characters of psychological complexity, which is why he turned repeatedly to the perusal of Byron's plays with a view to their presentation; Macready clearly sensed the affinity between Byron's artistry and his own unique skills. George Henry Lewes, a connoisseur of fine acting, thought Macready's greatest gift was his ability to 'express characters and . . . not like the melodramatic actor — [be] limited to *situations*'.[56] Lewes could cite no-one else amongst Macready's contemporaries who could show the gloomy, morose Werner as an object of increasing pathos, a view with which Dickens agreed: 'There is nothing I know, or can imagine, so exquisitely beautiful, so manly, noble, dignified, true, and brave, as that most exquisite and touching performance'.[57]

Byron's heroes — at least the four Macready chose to impersonate — are paradoxical figures: Werner, Faliero, Foscari Senior are all men who out of political necessity must keep their passionate souls hidden from view; in the depths of self they are hot-blooded, but circumstance requires them to appear cold, controlled, almost impersonal figures. Sardanapulus is something of an exception: he is an oriental voluptuary, but again there is a paradox in this in that his highly idiosyncratic way of life is discovered to be an expression of great courage and manliness of a unique kind; passion and sensuality are the essence of his nature but they are not the expression of an effeminate character, they are rather the tokens of a profound moral vision, for he aims to re-order his empire on pacifist, not militaristic values. His complete ease of being is a deliberate criticism of the traditional principles governing his world. The key to Macready's success in playing Byron's heroes is perhaps to be found in one of his *Journal* entries concerning what he felt to be a particularly satisfying performance as Werner: 'acted very well. Preserved an erect deportment in the midst of passion, and *let the mind act*' (my emphasis).[58] The mind, from what Marston writes of Macready, would clearly reveal itself through the actor's meticulously controlled voice intimating the play of emotions the body dare not express. All of Byron's tragic heroes are men struggling to preserve a personal, deeply felt integrity in a world they know to be dangerously corrupt and antipathetic to the values on which their inner lives are founded: it is in large measure their tragedy that their minds are richer than circumstance will ever allow them to show. Though Macready heavily cut and adapted Byron's texts, the plays as he performed them did stay true to Byron's conception in this respect at least. Audiences admired Macready's portayals and through him felt 'strong sympathy'[59] with Byron's protagonists; but the plays were never popular, except for *Werner*. Henry Crabb Robinson could give *Sardanapalus* only grudging respect, observing that 'it obtained more endurance than I expected'.[60] *Werner* was successful because it caught the mood of the theatrical times with its taste for domestic melodrama, for it is essentially a tragedy about paternal love, the discovery by Werner of a long-lost son at the very moment, because of Stralenheim's murder, when that son is lost irrevocably on ethical grounds. It touched the well-spring of Victorian sentiment as none of Byron's other plays did.[61]

Sardanapalus was destined to have a brilliant success in Victoria's reign in Charles Kean's production of 1853, when it received sixty-one performances in a season in which Boucicault's famous adaptation of *The Corsican Brothers* was given only fifty-five. The popularity was due, however, neither to Byron nor the acting (Lewes was astonished that 'any man accustomed to the stage [as Kean patently was] could speak the verse so ignorantly and *evade* expression so successfully').[62] The great attraction was, as with Bunn's *Manfred*, the scenery and not the play's challenging moral and political thesis. Layard had recently completed his excavations at Nineveh which had attracted considerable national interest. For Charles Kean with his passion for the educational value of authentic stage designs, costumes and props, the timing could not have been better. J. W. Cole, Kean's apologist, proudly asserted: 'until the present moment, it has been impossible to render Lord Byron's tragedy of *Sardanapalus* upon the stage with proper dramatic effect, because, until now we have known nothing of Assyrian architecture and costume'.[63] One has to admire the Alice-in-Wonderland illogic of that argument; but it captures certain mid-Victorian theatrical values exactly — values that were inimical not only to Byron's work but to all Romantic drama with its preoccupation with exploring the deeps of the mind.

Werner was to have one last and most prestigious performance in the nineteenth-century when Irving selected it as a benefit for the impecunious and dying Westland Marston on the afternoon of June 1st, 1887. It is a sign of Irving's consummate tact that he chose this play from the whole range of the dramatic repertoire to honour a man who as a fine theatre historian had celebrated Macready's skills with a remarkable sensitivity to the details of his art and so had ensured for posterity some insight into his genius. Any hopes that Irving might take the play into his standard repertoire, however, were quickly dashed as a consequence of the continuing success of the Lyceum's current attraction, *Faust*, and of Ellen Terry's antipathy to a play she thought might best be described as 'gloom, gloom, gloom', though she had to admit Irving himself had 'made it *intensely* interesting'.[64] Given the time and money Irving lavished on the production ('We rehearsed the play as carefully as if we were in for a long run'),[65] it might be supposed that he recognised in Werner a suitable role for his maturer years; a fitting vehicle it would have proved; but, whatever his private intentions with the play, they were, sadly, never realised.

This brings me to the present century and here I would like to appropriate Cole's rhetoric and argue that until the present moment, with the noble exception of Macready, it has indeed been impossible to render Lord Byron's tragedies upon the stage. He wrote, after Jeffrey had attacked the plays in the *Edinburgh Review*, that he was confident they 'may be trusted to Time', to a future when perhaps stage conditions and tastes would be different and more in sympathy with his own ends.[66] That that time has come seemed clear from a recent staging of *Marino Faliero* by Keith Hack at the Young Vic in October, 1982. A limited budget necessitated the choice of a studio theatre for the venture but necessity quickly proved a virtue: the Young Vic has an open, thrust stage; there was little attempt to disguise the basic structure of the background with scenery; the focus was exclusively on the actors and their subtlety of psychological portrayal. With this close proximity to the performers, one could relish to the full the tragic irony of Angiolina's failure to detect the waves of pent-up fury threatening to overwhelm her elderly husband, the Doge — she, a quiet, dutiful soul who clearly had never questioned authority in any form, could not begin to appreciate his depth of feeling or sense the potent danger of his condition, while he longs for a confidante with whom to open his heart but fears to sully her innocence. She proves in time to be made of sterner stuff than he imagines, leaping to his defence before the Council with a fire of attack born of genuine love for a husband whose life she dreads losing; his public dishonour means nothing to her by comparison. In these intimate staging conditions the actors had no difficulty in sustaining tension and dramatic momentum because our attention was rooted not so much in the situation as in the shifting nuances of feeling and insight. There were some lapses (such as an opening mime-sequence in which we watched Steno writing his slander against Marino as a drunken jape; and later the presentation of the last scene as a terrible memory passing through the consciousness of the near-catatonic Angiolina as she nursed Marino's severed head) [67] where the director succumbed to a kind of visual sensationalism that elsewhere he had firmly eliminated from his production; but these only served to highlight the general excellence of Hack's treatment. One detail deserves special mention — the handling of Lioni's long evocation of Venice seen by moonlight from his casement as he prepares wearily for bed. In the study this passage that opens Act IV might seem to suggest that the poet in Bryon has temporarily ousted the dramatist.[68] In performance the effect was quite other. Granted it is a moment of quiet rapture, an expression of sheer delight in the beauty of the night and of the place that can revive the man's jaded sensibility; but it is also a moment of stillness that the audience knows is soon to be rudely threatened: Lioni is savouring the preciousness of a moment that may well be his last. After the unrelieved psychological progression of the first three acts that has driven Marino to become the ally of Bertuccio's rebels, the pace suddenly and powerfully changes. Till now we have shared Marino's view of the situation, seen Venice and its patricians through his eyes and feelings only; Lioni offers a new perspective of feeling and awareness. The horizon widens from the personal and introspective controlling consciousness of Marino to a more objective appraisal of the political situation. The scene has a power analogous (in kind and structure, though obviously not in tone) with the arrival of the Porter in *Macbeth*. Far from being undramatic, the moment proved to be charged with a multiplicity of conflicing tones that changed only to intensify the tragic mood and drive.

The Romantics are often criticised for letting their plays tend too much towards the lyrical rather than the dramatic. Arguing from that basis, the *Times* in 1825 questioned: 'Who will not grieve a century hence that the *Foscari* was not written on a different system?' [69] On the strength of what Keith Hack's production of *Marino Faliero* revealed of Byron's dramatic sense, I would argue that one hundred and sixty years forward in time we are now in a position to value the dramatic excellence of *The Two Foscari* as perhaps Byron's finest achievement precisely because of its chosen system: its scrupulous adherence to the neo-classical Unities creates a mounting intensity in which, as in the Lioni episode, lyric *becomes* drama at its most vital. The younger Foscari has throughout the play frequent rhapsodic outbursts about the joys of riding in a gondola race in the Venetian sunshine, swimming or pursuing other energetic activities outdoors; his passionate hunger for the briefest of glimpses of the city through the windows as he is taken to and from his trials marvellously renders a mind and will desperate to avoid further exile at any cost; despite his terrible confines, that mind reaches out to luxuriate in the image of Venice as *home*. For him, Venice — even Venice known only from its courts and prisons — is his lifeblood. This may seem perverse, mad even — as his wife, Marina, consistently argues, but a passionate sense of place is the essence of the man enabling him to survive the most hideous of tortures and the grimmest dungeons with a spark of vitality unquenched. Threatened in time with the doom of exile, Foscari is suddenly quiet, the exuberance gone from him, drained by an all-consuming despair. As he is about to cross the threshold to leave for permanent exile, the passion surfaces once again and violently claims his life. In answer to his wife's question, 'How fare you?', he dies with the word, 'Well' on his lips. The Officer in charge of him observes, 'He's gone!' but old Foscari corrects the man for his insensitivity: 'He's free!' [70] There is superb irony and pathos in this conclusion as the son achieves his ambition: burial at home is better than a lingering non-life abroad. The lyricism of the young Foscari's role *is* the dramatic point; it is Byron's way of conveying the quality of the man's soul. As a dramatic device, it aids too the characterisation of Foscari Senior, the Doge. Like Faliero, Foscari is a man of feeling discovering that as Doge his nature must be contained, indeed subsumed within the duties of his office; he is to have no life outside his public status. He can be no *man* in the fullest sense of the word, as is made abundantly clear to him when he is required to sit inexorably in judgement on his own son and be the serenely objective arbiter of his fate. (That this cruel situation has been brought into being by Loredano as a calculated act of revenge against the old man defines the nature of Loredano's psyche too; every detail of the play carries psychological significance.) Marina cries out against her father-in-law's seeming impassivity; to her it is cruelly inhuman. As the play progresses and the son's lyricism waxes ever more passionate, one senses the cost of the suppression that old Foscari is imposing on himself; his will too must surely give way. In the event his control is maintained till the moment of his son's death when in an outburst of grief he flings himself on the corpse. He recovers his dignity in public and can even accept the demand for his abdication and his own demise with a calm sarcasm; and Loredano is robbed of ultimate triumph because he fails to see that the old man is absolute for death, having learned that his existence as Doge has been death-in-life. The son's passionate longings are the measure of all that the father suffers in secret; to sit in judgement on that son is to sit in judgement on his quintessential self. Far from being a weakness, the play's lyricism is a finely judged and sustained dramatic device that takes one straight to the core of Byron's psychological analysis as he discriminates in the play between a range of different kinds of obsession. *The Two Foscari* merits staging in Studio Theatre conditions which would seem to be the ideal environment for this style of theatre as has been proved by the success of Keith Hack's production of *Marino Faliero*, Debbie Sherwell's of *The Cenci* and three fine recent productions of Racine's *Andromaque, Britannicus* and *Bérénice*,[71] where in each case the intimacy of the theatre-space heightened the audience's imaginative engagement with the *inner* dynamic of the plays, their psychological and emotional structures, their 'underplot of character'.

* * * * *

Drama since Ibsen, Strindberg, Maeterlinck and Yeats has turned for its subject-matter increasingly inward — a tradition which poet-dramatists like Beckett and Pinter continue today. I would argue that Coleridge, Shelley and quintessentially Byron anticipate this tradition in a remarkably prophetic way and that, versed in such drama as we now are, we have a means of access to their plays denied to all but a select few of their contemporaries. We live in an age where small theatre-spaces allow the actor's art to be paramount and where the very proximity of performer to audience makes any hint of rant an embarrassment. Writers as disparate as Chekhov and Brecht have accustomed us to adopting more flexible responses to characters portrayed on stage than identification with heroes and loathing for villains. The Romantic poet-dramatists invite our imaginative engagement with character but not at the expense of our critical faculties: effecting just discriminations is of the essence of Coleridge's dramatic artistry and of Shelley's and Byron's. They encourage us to wonder at the intricate workings of the human mind and the unique quality of each character's sensibility and to share their fascination with the ways that the mind and the sensibility can shape an individual's destiny. To an astonishing degree Byron in particular sensed, if not the precise shape of things to come, at least that the whirligig of time would bring in its revenges on the theatre practice of his day. He was right to trust to the future and the burden rests now with us not to betray his confidence.

NOTES

1. THE ROMANTIC POET AND THE STAGE
Timothy Webb

1 *Collected Letters of Samuel Taylor Coleridge*, edited by Earl Leslie Griggs, 6 vols (Oxford, 1956-71), IV, 721; *Byron's Letters and Journals*, edited by Leslie A. Marchand, 12 vols (London, 1974-82), IV, 115; *Shelley's Poetry and Prose*, edited by Donald H. Reiman and Sharon B. Powers (New York, 1977), 492; *The Complete Works of William Hazlitt*, edited by P. P. Howe, 21 vols (London and Toronto, 1930-34), XVIII, 302.
2 W. B. Yeats, *Memoirs: Autobiography — First Draft, Journal*, edited by Denis Donoghue (London, 1972), 151.
3 Hazlitt, *Works*, XVIII, 308.
4 Yeats, *Memoirs*, 151-52.
5 Coleridge, *Letters*, II, 1033.
6 *Ibid*, III, 428; *Biographia Literaria*, edited by James Engell and W. Jackson Bate, 2 vols (London and Princeton, N.J., 1982), II, 19; *The Notebooks of Samuel Taylor Coleridge*, edited by Kathleen Coburn, 3 vols (New York and London, 1957—), III, 4117.
7 See Preface to *The Excursion* (1814) l. 40.
8 *Biographia Literaria*, II, 135.
9 *The Prelude* (1805), X.54-77, 377-81.
10 *Wordsworth's Poetical Works*, Poems Written in Early Youth, edited by E. De Selincourt (Oxford, 1940), 342-43.
11 Hazlitt, *Works*, IV, 113.
12 For a detailed exposition, see G. Wilson Knight, *Byron and Shakespeare* (London, 1966).
13 Poems Written in Early Youth, 343.
14 *The Complete Poetical Works of Samuel Taylor Coleridge*, edited by E. H. Coleridge, 2 vols (Oxford, 1912), II, 495.
15 *The Complete Writings of Thomas Paine*, edited by P. S. Foner (New York, 1945), I, 258-68, cited in Peter H. Melvin 'Burke on Theatricality and Revolution', *Journal of the History of Ideas*, 36 (1975), 447-68.
16 *Complete Poetical Works*, II, 724-25.
17 Coleridge, *Letters*, I, 358.
18 *Ibid*, I, 356.
19 *Ibid*, III, 428; *Preface, Complete Poetical Works*, II, 812-15.
20 Coleridge, *Letters*, III, 427.
21 *Complete Poetical Works*, II, 812.
22 Coleridge, *Letters*, III, 428, 432.
23 *Ibid*, IV, 591.
24 *Ibid*, IV, 721.
25 For details of these and other performances, see Chapter Four and Margaret J. Howell, *Byron Tonight: A Poet's Plays on the Nineteenth Century Stage* (Windlesham, 1982).
26 *The Letters of Percy Bysshe Shelley*, edited by F. L. Jones, 2 vols (Oxford, 1964), II, 8.

27 *The Perfect Wagnerite, Major Critical Essays* (London, [1932] reprinted 1947), 218; for 'lyrical drama', see Ronald Tetreault, 'Shelley and the Opera', E.L.H., 48 (1981), 144-71.
28 Shelley, *Letters*, II, 96, 102, 174, 178, 102, 181; *Poetical Works*, 337; *Letters*, II, 102, 219.
29 *Letters*, II, 219-20.
30 *The Complete Poetical Works of Percy Bysshe Shelley*, edited by Thomas Hutchinson, corrected by G. M. Matthews (London, 1970), 482.
31 For a detailed account of these translations, see Timothy Webb, *The Violet in the Crucible: Shelley and Translation* (Oxford, 1976).
32 Newman Ivey White, *Shelley*, 2 vols (New York, 1940), I, 575, n.65.
33 Shelley, *Letters*, II, 8.
34 *The Letters of John Keats: 1814-1821* edited by Hyder E. Rollins, 2 vols (Cambridge, Mass., 1958), II, 157.
35 *The Keats Circle*, edited by Hyder E. Rollins, 2 vols (Cambridge, Mass., 1965), II, 66-67.
36 Coleridge, *Notebooks*, II, 2573; see also III, 3654.
37 Coleridge, *Letters*, III, 430-31.
38 *Henry Crabb Robinson on Books and their Writers*, edited by Edith J. Morley, 3 vols (London, 1938), I, 117-18.
39 Coleridge, *Letters*, I, 185.
40 Coleridge, *Letters*, IV, 620.
41 Coleridge, *Letters*, III, 421; *Notebooks*, II, 2064; *Letters*, III, 422.
42 Coleridge, *Letters*, IV, 590, 598-99; 'Notes on the History Plays', *Coleridge's Shakespearean Criticism*, edited by T. M. Raysor, second edition, 2 vols (London and New York, 1960), I, 129.
43 *Shakespearean Criticism*, II, 231.
44 Coleridge, *Letters*, IV, 590-91, 599.
45 Hazlitt, *Works*, V, 264-66.
46 *Ibid*, V, 222.
47 Coleridge, *Letters*, IV, 606.
48 Coleridge, *Notebooks*, I, 871; *Complete Poetical Works*, II, 1060-73.
49 *Notebooks*, II, 2692.
50 *Ibid*, III, 4245 and n; see also I, 1723n., II, 2692n.
51 Hazlitt, *Works*, XVIII, 323; Coleridge, *Letters*, IV, 605.
52 Keats, *Letters*, II, 186.
53 *Ibid*, II, 234.
54 *The Poetical Works and Other Writings of John Keats*, edited by H. B. Forman, revised by M. B. Forman, 8 vols, (London, 1938-39), V, 229-30.
55 Byron, *Letters and Journals*, IV, 115.
56 *Poetical Works and Other Writings*, V, 230-31.
57 Robert Gittings, *John Keats* (London, 1968, revised edition 1970), 175; Keats, *Letters*, I, 193.
58 Keats, *Letters*, II, 139. See Byron, *Letters and Journals*, IV, 67: 'he is a wonder ... & will run Kemble hard — his style is quite new — or rather *renewed* — being that of Nature'.
59 Preface to *Prometheus Unbound*, *Shelley's Poetry and Prose*, 134.
60 *Defence of Poetry*, *Shelley's Poetry and Prose*, 491-92.
61 Translated by John Black; see Timothy Webb, *English Romantic Hellenism 1700-1824* (Manchester, 1982), 211-19.
62 *The Rambler*, Number 168.
63 *Notebooks*, III, 3952.
64 Coleridge, *Letters*, IV, 598.
65 *Memoirs of Shelley and other Essays and Reviews*, edited by Howard Mills

(London, 1970), 46; Mary Shelley noted: 'He was not a playgoer, being of such fastidious taste that he was easily disgusted by the bad filling-up of the inferior parts' (*Poetical Works*, 336).
66 Shelley, *Letters*, II, 8; *Shelley's Poetry and Prose*, 391.
67 Coleridge, *Letters*, IV, 720.
68 *Ibid*, IV, 720.
69 Coleridge, *Letters*, I, 653.
70 'An Essay . . .', *Dramatic Essays: Leigh Hunt*, edited by William Archer and Robert W. Lowe (London, 1894), 137-38.
71 *English Plays of the Nineteenth-Century*, III. Comedies, edited by Michael R. Booth (Oxford, 1973), 153.
72 Leigh Hunt, *Critical Essays on the Performers of the London Theatres*, (London, 1807), 81.
73 Coleridge, *Letters*, III, 500-01.
74 *Ibid*, III, 500.
75 Peacock, *Memoirs*, 69.
76 *Ibid*, 45.
77 *Ibid*, 46.
78 *Defence of Poetry, Shelley's Poetry and Prose*, 491.
79 *Ibid*, 489.
80 Preface to *Prometheus Unbound, Ibid*, 135.
81 Michael R. Booth, 'The Social and Literary Context', *The Revels History of Drama in English*, 7 vols (London, 1975), VI, 4.
82 *Autobiography*, edited by J. E. Morpurgo (London, 1949), 136.
83 Leigh Hunt, 'Retrospect of the Theatre', *The Reflector* (1811), 233-34.
84 *Ibid*, 234.
85 See Ronald Paulson, *Popular and Polite Art in the Age of Hogarth and Fielding* (Notre Dame and London, 1979), 115-34.
86 *The Revels History of Drama in English*, VI, Plate 9a.
87 For further details, see Joseph Donohue, 'The London Theatre at the End of the Eighteenth Century' in *The London Theatre World, 1660-1800*, edited by Robert D. Hume (Carbondale and Edwardsville, 1980), 337-70.
88 Cited from *Essays on Chivalry, Romance, and the Drama* (London, n.d.), 224.
89 See Sybil Rosenfeld, *Georgian Scene Painters and Scene Painting* (Cambridge, 1981).
90 Hazlitt, *Works*, V, 275.
91 *Ibid*, V, 231.
92 *The Works of Charles and Mary Lamb*, edited by E. V. Lucas, 7 vols (London, 1903-05), I, 110.
93 *Ibid*.
94 Hazlitt, *Works*, V, 276.
95 *Shakespeare Criticism*, II, 230-31; Coleridge *Letters*, IV, 720.
96 See W. Moelwyn Merchant, *Shakespeare and the Artist* (London, 1959), Chapter 5.
97 Letter of 21 December 1833 cited from *Lamb as Critic*, edited by Roy Park (London, 1980), 348.
98 S. T. Coleridge, *Table Talk*, edited by T. Ashe (London, 1888), 25; J. Fitzgerald Molloy, *The Life and Adventures of Edmund Kean* (London, 1888), I, 248; Byron, *Letters and Journals*, IV, 115; Hazlitt, *Works*, V, 209.
99 Hazlitt, *Works*, V, 184.
100 Coleridge, *Shakespearean Criticism*, II, 230, 68.
101 Lamb, *Works*, I, 111, 104.
102 *Leigh Hunt's Dramatic Criticism 1808-1831*, edited by Lawrence H. Houtchens and Carolyn W. Houtchens (New York, 1949), 47-48.

103 *Ibid*, 50.
104 W. C. Oulton, *A History of the Theatres of London . . . from the Year 1795 to 1817 inclusive* (London, 1817), II, 274 (see 266), cited in *Revels History*, VI, 110.
105 Lord Byron, *The Complete Poetical Works*, edited by Jerome J. McGann, 5 vols (Oxford, 1980-86), III, 20-21.
106 Byron, *Letters and Journals*, IX, 35-36.
107 *Ibid*, IV, 290.
108 *Ibid*, IV, 290-1.
109 *Medwin's Conversations of Lord Byron*, edited by Ernest J. Lovell, Jr, (Princeton, N.J., 1966), 93.
110 Marginal note in a letter of 15 June 1815 cited in *Revels History*, VI, 194-95.
111 Byron, *Letters and Journals*, VIII, 23.
112 *Ibid*, VIII, 57.
113 *Ibid*, VIII, 78.
114 *Ibid*, V, 196. And see David Erdman, 'Byron's Stage Fright: The History of his Ambition and Fear of Writing for the Stage', *E.L.H.* 6 (1939), 219-43.
115 Byron, *Letters and Journals*, VIII, 186-87.
116 Keats, *Letters*, II, 322-23. See Shelley's claim in the *Preface*: 'I have avoided with great care in writing this play the introduction of what is commonly called mere poetry' (*Shelley's Poetry and Prose*, 241).
117 *Medwin's Conversations*, 94.
118 Byron, *Letters and Journals*, VII, 184.
119 *Ibid*, VIII, 67.
120 *Medwin's Conversations*, 120; see Byron's *Preface*.

2. THE DRAMAS OF BYRON
Giorgio Melchiori

1 *Byron's Letters and Journals*, edited by Leslie A. Marchand, 12 volumes (London, 1973-82), V, 170.
2 *The Poetical Works of Lord Byron*, (Oxford Standard Authors, London, 1904; reprinted, 1957), 453.
3 *Byron's Letters and Journals*, V, 203.
4 *The Poetical Works of Lord Byron*, 408.
5 *Ibid*.
6 *Ibid*, 453.
7 *Ibid*, 520.
8 *Ibid*.
9 *Ibid*, 521.
10 Genesis, VI. ii.
11 *The Poetical Works of Lord Byron*, 403. (*Manfred*, III. ii. 4-7.)
12 *Ibid*, 560.
13 *Ibid*.
14 *Ibid*.
15 *Ibid*, 390. (*Manfred*, I. i. 1-27.)
16 *Byron's Letters and Journals*, V, 170.
17 *Ibid*.
18 *Ibid*, 188.
19 *Ibid*. VI, 7.
20 W. B. Yeats, 'Lapis Lazuli', *Collected Poems*, (Second Edition, London, 1950; reprinted, 1960) 338.
21 *Byron's Letters and Journals*, VII, 182.
22 *Ibid*, VI, 206.
23 James Joyce, *A Portrait of the Artist as a Young Man*, edited by C. G. Anderson,

(New York, 1964), 80-82.
24 Cited by Richard Ellmann, *James Joyce*, (London and New York, 1959), 640.
25 *The Poetical Works of Lord Byron*, 605.
26 *Ibid*, 623.
27 *Ibid*, 620. (*The Deformed Transformed*, Part II, Scene iii. 30-3.)
28 *Ibid*, 621. (II. iii. 75-8.)

3. SHELLEYAN DRAMA
Stuart Curran

1 The best treatment of the implications for dramatic form embodied in this style of acting is in Joseph Donohue, *Dramatic Character in the English Romantic Age* (Princeton, 1970). For specific links to Shelley's dramatic practices, see my *Shelley's 'Cenci': Scorpions Ringed with Fire*, (Princeton, 1970), and Ronald Tetrault's 'Shelley at the Opera', *E.L.H.*, 48 (1981), 144-71.
2 See Stuart Curran, *Shelley's Annus Mirabilis: The Maturing of an Epic Vision*, (San Marino, California, 1975), 187-92.
3 See 'Shelley and the Improvvisatore Sgricci: An Unpublished Review', *Keats-Shelley Memorial Bulletin*, 32, (1981). 19-29; also Earl Wasserman, *Shelley: A Critical Reading*, (Baltimore, 1971), 378-80.
4 For this text and that of Shelley's major poems I rely on *Shelley's Poetry and Prose*, edited by Donald H. Reiman and Sharon B. Powers, (New York, 1977): 'A Defence of Poetry', 491-92. For the fragment of *Charles the First*, I use the text of the Thomas Hutchison edition of *Shelley's Complete Poems*, (Oxford, 1905), whose corruptions do not affect the present argument. The full text of the passage quoted from *A Defence of Poetry* is given in Chapter One on pages 24-25.
5 *Shelley's Poetry and Prose*, 241.
6 *Ibid*, 240.
7 *Ibid*, 491.
8 *Ibid*, 490.
9 The best treatment of this drama, concentrating on it as a neo-Shakespearean History Play, is by R. B. Woodings, 'A Devil of a Nut to Crack: Shelley's *Charles the First*', *Studia Neophilogica*, 11 (1968), 216-37; see also his 'Shelley's Sources for *Charles the First*', *Modern Language Review*, 64, (1969), 267-75. Both essays contain otherwise unavailable manuscript material.
10 *Charles the First*, I. i. 31-7.
11 This fragment was first called to our attention by Neville Rogers in *Shelley at Work*, (Oxford, 1956); it is placed within the context of Shelley's extensive thinking about Calderón in Timothy Webb, *The Violet in the Crucible: Shelley and Translation*, (Oxford, 1976) 221, from which I quote.
12 *Charles the First*, I. ii. 94.
13 *Ibid*, I. ii. 360-62.
14 *Prometheus Unbound*, II. i. 116-17.
15 *Hellas*, ll. 795-802.
16 The most salient discussion of the dramatic properties of *Hellas* is that of Constance Walker, 'The Urn of Bitter Prophecy: Antithetical Patterns in *Hellas*', *Keats-Shelley Memorial Bulletin*, 33 (1982), 36-48.
17 *Prometheus Unbound*, II. iv. 9-11.
18 *Hellas*, ll. 696-703.

4. ROMANTIC DRAMA IN PERFORMANCE
Richard Allen Cave

1 Cited in *Shelley: The Critical Heritage*, edited by James E. Barcus, (London, 1975), 175.

2 *The Letters of Percy Bysshe Shelley*, edited by Frederick L. Jones, 2 volumes, (Oxford, 1964), II, 102. The letter is dated July, 1819.
3 *Byron's Letters and Journals*. Edited by Leslie A. Marchand, 12 volumes, (London, 1973-82), V, 170.
4 *Ibid*, 188.
5 A canvas inspired by the poem, *Manfred on the Jungfrau*, was completed by Martin c. 1826; a watercolour version of 1837 is now in the collection of the Birmingham City Art Gallery.
6 J. Westland Marston, *Our Recent Actors*, (New edition, London, 1890), 9.
7 *The London Theatre 1811-1866. Selections from the diary of Henry Crabb Robinson*, edited by Eluned Brown, (The Society for Theatre Research, London, 1966), 144. Robinson continues: 'There must be some merit in this poem since Goethe admired it — but as a drama nothing could be worse . . . It is a sort of Don Juan without wit or fun or character — no relief — no variety. . . . The performance of such a thing proves something like the extinction of drama as such — it should be called a show in which grand pictures are explained by words . . .'
8 *Our Recent Actors*, 9. Henry Crabb Robinson was not as impressed as the young Marston: 'The invocations in lyric verse sounded like doggerel though great pains were taken by the declaimer to throw dignity and tragic effect into the recitation' (*The London Theatre 1811-1866*, 144-45).
9 *Our Recent Actors*, 9-10.
10 *Ibid*, 11-12.
11 *The Poetical Works of Lord Byron*, (Oxford Standard Authors, London, 1904; reprinted, 1957), 491.
12 Anne Barton: ' "A light to lesson ages" — Byron's Political Plays', *Byron. A Symposium*, edited by John D. Jump, (London, 1975), 138-161.
13 *Byron's Letters and Journals*, VI, 206. See Chapter II, 57.
14 *Ibid*, 217.
15 *Ibid*, IX, 31.
16 Thomas Medwin, *Conversations of Lord Byron*, (London, 1824), I, 194.
17 See Wordsworth's revised Preface to the *Lyrical Ballads* of 1802.
18 *Collected Letters of Samuel Taylor Coleridge*, edited by E. L. Griggs, 6 volumes, (Oxford, 1956-71), III, 437.
19 *Ibid*, 433-4.
20 Cited in *Coleridge — The Critical Heritage*, edited by J. R. de J. Jackson, (London, 1970), 115.
21 *Collected Letters of Samuel Taylor Coleridge*, III, 436.
22 *Ibid*, 434.
23 *Ibid*.
24 Cited in *Coleridge — The Critical Heritage*, 138-9.
25 *Literary Gazette*, April 1, 1820. Cited in *Shelley — The Critical Heritage*, 164.
26 See *The Complete Poetical Works of Percy Bysshe Shelley*, edited by Thomas Hutchinson, (London, 1905; reprinted, 1960), 277. For a fuller discussion of this point see my article, '*The Cenci* in performance' *The Keats-Shelley Memorial Bulletin*, XXXVI, (Heslington, York, 1985), 114.
27 *The Times* carried a review of the Shelley Society's production on Saturday May 8, 1886, 14.
28 James Agate, *At Half-Past Eight (Essays of the Theatre 1921-1922)*, (London, 1923), 190.
29 *The Times*, April 30, 1959, 3.
30 At the Orange Tree Theatre, Richmond in February, 1983.
31 *The Complete Poetical Works of Percy Bysshe Shelley*, 332.

32 *Henry Crabb Robinson on Books and Their Writers*, edited by Edith J. Morley. (London, 1938), II, 652.
33 *The London Figaro*, May 15, 1886, 14.
34 *The Times*, May 8, 1886, 14.
35 *At Half-Past Eight*, 188.
36 *Ibid*, 191.
37 I have attempted to reconstruct Miss Jefford's interpretation of the role of Beatrice Cenci from a selection of reviews pasted in the Scrapbooks of the Library of the British Theatre Association and have relied chiefly on those taken from *The Times* and *The Daily Telegraph*. Not all the reviews, however, are properly annotated as to their source.
38 For discussion of a different way of handling the *Macbeth* 'echoes' see my article, cited above, '*The Cenci* in performance'.
39 *The Times*, April 30, 1959, 3.
40 See the stage directions for Act One, Scene Three (126), Act Three, Scene Two (142-3), and Act Four Scene One (144-5) in *Antonin Artaud: The Collected Works*, translated by Victor Corti, (London, 1974).
41 *Ibid*, 151.
42 Cited in *Byron — The Critical Heritage*, edited by Andrew Rutherford, (London, 1970), 217.
43 See, for example, Byron's observation that *Bertram* is 'of great & singular merit as a composition & capable — we hope — with some alterations & omissions — of being adapted even to the *present* state of the Stage — which is not the most encouraging to men of talent. — What it seems to want for this purpose is *lowering* (in some of the Scenes) — this for the sake of the physical powers of the actor — as well as to relieve the attention of an audience — no performer could support the tone & effort of continual & sustained passion through five acts' (*Byron's Letters and Journals*, IV, 336).
44 *Ibid*, VIII, 151.
45 Anne Barton contends persuasively that Byron actually followed the fortunes of the Elliston production of *Marino Faliero* more keenly than he pretended and that secretly he hoped for success as a dramatist.
46 Cited from Kelly's *Reminiscences*, (II, 317) by Marchand in *Byron's Letters and Journals*, IV, 115.
47 *Ibid*, IV, 216.
48 *Drury Lane Journal: Selections from James Winston's Diaries 1819-1827*, edited by A. L. Nelson and G. B. Cross, (The Society for Theatre Research, London, 1974), 70.
49 This was written specifically of *The Two Foscari* but in a context where Byron is generalising about the dramatic method he employs in all his tragedies. See *Byron's Letters and Journals*, VIII, 218.
50 *Our Recent Actors*, 65.
51 *Ibid*, 67.
52 *Ibid*, 28-9.
53 *Ibid*, 60.
54 *Ibid*, 63.
55 See the entry for March 23, 1836, headed 'Plymouth': 'My endeavour to act Werner well was completely frustrated. The whole play was acted very indifferently; Josephine was dressed like a flower-girl for a fancy ball; Idenstein, Fritz, Stralenheim all bad — Gabor not good — but Ulric was beyond all power of description — winking with his eyes, then starting, and looking very fine, mysterious, and assassin-like — then as flippant as a man-milliner. He quite *paralysed* me. I contended with this oppressive incubus,

and made some effect, but the heart was absent'. *The Journal of William Charles Macready 1832-1851*, edited by J. C. Trewin, (London, 1967), 59.
56 George Henry Lewes, *On Actors and the Art of Acting*, (London, 1875), 37.
57 *The Letters of Charles Dickens*, (The Pilgrim Edition) Volume 2: 1840-1847, edited by Madeleine House and Graham Storey, (Oxford, 1969), 280.
58 *The Journal of William Charles Macready*, 3.
59 *Ibid*, 183. Macready was playing *Marino Faliero* for his Benefit night on May 20, 1842: '. . . the interest of the play grew upon the audience, and the curtain fell upon the death of Faliero with their strong sympathy'.
60 *The London Theatre 1811-1866*, 141.
61 Samuel Phelps, who considered himself in many ways the inheritor of Macready's mantle, continued to play Werner at Sadlers Wells — 'eleven times during eighteen seasons' according to Margaret Howell, *Byron Tonight*, (Windlesham, 1982), 176 — and elsewhere until his retirement in 1860. It was not, however, one of his major achievements and he never numbered the role as Macready did amongst his first five favourites. Howell also records provincial performances of *Werner* in Bristol as late as 1869 (*Byron Tonight*, 162).
62 John Forster and George Henry Lewes, *Dramatic Essays*, edited by William Archer and Robert W. Lowe, (London, 1896), 251. Lewes accused Kean of 'uttering the words in tones directly contrary to the sense'.
63 J. W. Cole, *The Life and Theatrical Times of Charles Kean*, (Second edition, London, 1870), II, 59. Cole continues by remarking that Byron 'would have been taught, too, that the tribunal he so earnestly prayed deliverance from, is never slow to acknowledge the supremacy of genius, when clothed in appropriate garb and attended by its indispensable accessories'. Henry Crabb Robinson, recalling his dislike of Macready's production, observed: '. . . saw *Sardanapalus* a second time. It wearied me less than I expected' (*The London Theatre 1811-1866*, 197). George Henry Lewes tartly questioned: 'Was Byron only a pretext for a panorama?'
64 *Ellen Terry's Memoirs*, edited by Edith Craig and Christopher St. John, (London, 1933), 189.
65 *Ibid*.
66 *Byron's Letters and Journals*, IX, 159.
67 It is interesting that Macready also played a conclusion different from that Byron conceived and one that, similar to Hack's, placed the focus at the end on Angiolina: as the executioner was about to strike off the Doge's head, Angiolina was heard crying without; she entered, asserting 'I will not be with-held; my lord, my husb—'; the Senators threw themselves before and about Marino concealing the moment of his death; a bell tolled; Angiolina shrieked and fell as the curtain descended.
68 *The Poetical Works of Lord Byron*, 434-5. The speech lasts some 111 lines.
69 From a scrapbook of newspaper cuttings relating to Drury Lane Theatre 1777-1834 in the British Library, Catalogue ref. Th. Cts. 40.
70 *The Poetical Works of Lord Byron*, 512. (IV. i. 192-3.)
71 *Andromaque* was staged at the Donmar Theatre in January, 1985; *Britannicus* and *Bérénice* at the Lyric Theatre Studio, Hammersmith, in May, 1981 and May, 1982 respectively.

BIBLIOGRAPHY

compiled by Christina Gee and Judith Knight

GENERAL

BAUM, Joan Mandell. *The Theatrical compositions of the major English Romantic poets.* Salzburg: Institut für Anglistik und Americanistik, University of Salzburg, 1980. (Salzburg Studies in English Literature: Poetic Drama & Poetic Theory, No. 57).

BOOTH, Michael R. *English Melodrama.* London: Herbert Jenkins, 1965.

BURTON, E[rnest] J[ames]. *The British Theatre: its repertory and practice, 1100 – 1900 A.D.* London: Herbert Jenkins, 1960.

BRUGGER, Ilse M. de. *Breve historia del teatro inglés.* Buenos Aires: Editorial Nova, 1959.

CARLISLE, Carol J. 'The Nineteenth century actors versus the closet critics of Shakespeare', *Studies in Philology*, LI, October 1954, pp. 599-615.

DONOHUE, Joseph W., Jr. *Dramatic character in the English Romantic age.* Princeton: Princeton University, 1970.

EHRSTINE, John W. 'The Drama and Romantic Theory: The Cloudy Symbols of High Romance', *Research Studies*, XXXIV, June 1966, pp. 85-106.

FLETCHER, Richard M. *English Romantic Drama 1795-1843: A critical history.* New York: Exposition, 1966.

GAULL, Marilyn. 'Romantic Theatre', *Wordsworth Circle*, XIV, no. 4, pp. 255-263.

HEWITT, Barnard. *History of the theatre from 1800 to the present.* New York: Random House, 1970.

JACOBUS, Mary. ' "That great stage where Senators perform": *Macbeth* and the politics of Romantic theater', *Studies in Romanticism*, 22, Fall 1983, pp. 353-387.

KAUVAR, Gerald B. and Gerald C. SORENSON, comps. *Nineteenth-Century English Verse Drama.* Rutherford, N.J.: Fairleigh Dickinson University, 1973.

MANDER, Raymond and Joe MITCHENSON. *A Picture History of the British Theatre.* London: Hulton, 1957.

NAVONE, John. 'The Italian Devils of Anglo-Saxon Literature', *New Blackfriars*, 55, February 1974, pp. 68-77.

NICOLL, Allardyce. *A History of English Drama: 1600-1900*. Vol. IV: *Early Nineteenth Century Drama: 1800-1850*. Cambridge: Cambridge University Press, 1955.

NICOLL, Allardyce. *A History of English Drama 1660-1900*. Vol VI: *A Short Title Alphabetical Catalogue of Plays produced or printed in England from 1600-1900*. Cambridge: Cambridge University Press, 1959.

OTTEN, Terry. *The Deserted Stage: the search for dramatic form in nineteenth century England*. Athens: Ohio University, 1972.

RAIZIS, M. Byron. *From Caucasus to Pittsburgh: The Prometheus theme in British and American poetry*. Athens: Gnosis, 1982.

RICHARDS, Kenneth and Peter THOMSON eds. *Essays on nineteenth century British theatre: The proceedings of a symposium sponsored by Manchester University Department of Drama*. London: Methuen; New York: Barnes and Noble, 1971.

ROWELL, George. *The Victorian Theatre, a survey*. London: Oxford, 1956.

RULFS, Donald J. 'The Romantic writers and Edmund Kean', *Modern Language Quarterly*, XI, December 1950, pp. 425-437.

STEINER, George. *The death of tragedy*. New York: Knopf, 1961.

STRATMAN, Carl J. 'English tragedy: 1819-1823', *Philological Quarterly*, XLI, April 1962, pp. 465-474.

TREWIN, J. C. *The night has been unruly*. London: Hale, 1957.

TREWIN, J. C. 'The Romantic poets and the theatre', *Keats-Shelley Memorial Bulletin*, 20, 1969, pp. 21-30.

TREWIN, J. C. *Verse drama since 1800*. Cambridge: Cambridge University for the National Book League, 1956. (Readers Guides. Second Series, no. 8.)

WEARING, J. P. 'Nineteenth Century Theatre Research: a bibliography for 1979', *Nineteenth Century Theatre Research*, 10, Winter 1982, pp. 93-109.

LORD BYRON

ANIKST, A. 'Byron as dramatist', in *Lord Byron: Plays: translated from the English*. Moscow: Iskusstvo, 1959, pp. 5-21.

ASHE, Dora J. 'Byron's alleged part in the production of Coleridge's "Remorse"', *Notes and Queries*, CXCVIII, January 1953, pp. 33-36.

ASHTON, Thomas L. '*Marino Faliero*: Byron's "Poetry of Politics" ', *Studies in Romanticism*, 13, Winter 1974, pp. 1-13.
BALL, Patricia M. 'Byronic Drama', *Orpheus*, II, January-May 1955, pp. 25-31
BARKER, Kathleen M. D. 'The first English performance of Byron's "Werner" ', *Modern Philology*, LXVI, May 1969, pp. 342-344.
BARTON, Anne. ' "A light to lesson ages" — Byron's Political Plays' in *Byron. A Symposium*, edited by J. D. Jump, London, 1975, pp. 138-161.
BEBBINGTON, W. G. '*The Two Foscari*', *English*, IX, Autumn 1953, pp. 201-206.
BAUER, N. Stephen. 'Byron's Doubting Cain', *South Atlantic Bulletin*, 39, May 1974, pp. 80-88.
BIDNEY, Martin. 'Cain and The Ghost of Abel: Contexts for understanding Blake's response to Byron', *Blake Studies*, 8, no. 2, 1979, pp. 145-165.
BÜCHI, Adolf. *Byrons 'Manfred' und die historischen Dramen*. Bern: Francke, 1972. (Schweizer Anglistische Arbeiten: Swiss Studies in English, vol. 68.)
BUTLER, Maria Hogan. 'An examination of Byron's revision of "Manfred", Act III', *Studies in Philology*, LX, October, 1963, pp. 627-636.
BYRON, Lord. *Cain*; translated into German by Wilhelm Leyhausen. Performed at the university of Zurich by the Akademische Theatergruppe Zurich in Spring 1951.
BYRON, Lord. *Caino*; con introd. e note di Giuseppe de Lorenzo. Traduzione di Ferdinando Milone. Firenze: Sansoni, 1942.
BYRON, Lord. *Lord Byron's 'Cain': Twelve essays and a text with variants and annotations.* ed. by Truman Guy Steffan. Austin and London: University of Texas, 1969.
BYRON, Lord. 'Lord Byron's *Cain* produced in Lucerne', *The Times*, 12 April 1960, p. 6.
BYRON, Lord. *Manfred*: Ein Dramat Gedicht. [Manfred: a dramatic poem]. Eds. Helmut Viebrock and Eileen Volhard; translated by Otto Gildemeister. Frankfurt a.M.: Heinrich-Heine-Verlag, 1969.
BYRON, Lord. *Manfredo*, poema dramatico en verso castellano por Jose Alacala Galiano. Prologo de Juan Valera. Montevideo: C. Garcia, 1943.

BYRON, Lord. *Werner, A tragedy.* A facsimile of the acting version of William Charles Macready. Ed. by Martin Spevack. Munich: W. Fink, 1970.

CALLAND, Fred. 'Revival of *Manfred* at Mershon [auditorium] is a memorable experience', *Citizen-Journal* (Columbus, Ohio), 6 April 1963.

CHEW, Samuel C. Jr. *The Dramas of Lord Byron: a critical study.* New York, Russell & Russell, 1964. First published 1915.

CLANCY, Charles J. 'Death and love in Byron's "Sardanapalus" ', *Byron Journal*, 10, 1982, pp. 55-71.

CLAVERIA, Carlos. *Temas de Unamuno.* Madrid: Gredos, 1953.

COOKE, M. G. 'The restoration ethos of Byron's classical plays', *PMLA*, LXXIX, December 1964, pp. 569-578.

DAMICO, Helen. 'The Stage history of *Werner*', *Nineteenth Century Theatre Research*, 3, Autumn 1975, pp. 63-81.

DEDEYAN, Charles. 'Le thème de Faust: Le préromantisme', *La revue des lettres modernes*, December 1955, pp. 211-256 and January 1956, pp. 49-96.

DEDEYAN, Charles. *Le thème de Faust dans la litterature européenne: Le préromantisme.* Paris: Lettres modernes, 1955.

DIBDIN, Charles. *Memoirs of Charles Dibdin the younger.* Ed. by George Speaight. London: Society for Theatre Research, 1956.

DOBBS, Brian. *Drury Lane: Three centuries of the Theatre Royal, 1663-1971.* London: Cassell, 1972.

EGGENSCHWILER, David. 'The tragic and the comic rhythms of *Manfred*', *Studies in Romanticism*, 13, Winter 1974, pp. 63-77.

EVANS, Bertrand. 'Manfred's remorse and dramatic tradition', *PMLA*, 62, 1947, pp. 752-774.

FARWELL, Beatrice. 'Sources for Delacroix's *Death of Sardanapalus*', *Art Bulletin*, XL, March 1958, pp. 66-71.

FRYKMAN, Erik. 'Lucifer och Kain: Byrons och Arthur Millers', [Lucifer and Cain: Byron's and Arthur Miller's], *Artes* (Stockholm), 5, no. 4, 1979, pp. 119-127.

GORCHAKOV, Nikolai A. *The theater in Soviet Russia.* Translated by Edgar Lehrman. New York: Columbia University, 1957. [Moscow Art Theatre's production of *Cain* discussed.]

HACHIYA, Akio. 'Byron's *Cain* and the Bible', *Foreign Literary Studies of Osaka Women's College*, no. 15, February 1963, pp. 1-10.

HARDWICK, J. M. D. ed. *Emigrant in motley: the journey of Charles and Ellen Kean . . . in Australia and America, as told in their hitherto* unpublished letters.... London: Rockcliff, 1954. [Includes references to Kean's revival of *Sardanapalus* in 1853.]

HELLENIKE DEMIOURGIA. *Obras escogidas: Don Juan; Childe Harold; El Corsario; Cain; Sardanapalo; Manfredo*. Translated by E. Villalva and Jose Alcala Galiano. Buenos Aires: Atenec, 1951.

HOWARTH, R. G. *A pot of gilly-flowers: studies and notes*. Cape Town: The Author, 1964. [Includes 'Byron as dramatist'].

HOWELL, Margaret J. *Byron tonight: a poet's plays on the nineteenth century stage*. Windlesham, Surrey: Springwood Books, 1982.

HOWELL, Margaret J. 'Sardanapalus', *Byron Journal*, no. 2, 1974, pp. 42-53.

KAHN, Arthur D. 'Seneca and Sardanapalus: Byron the Don Quixote of Neo-classicism', *Studies in Philology*, 66, July 1969, pp. 654-671.

KELSALL, Malcolm. 'Goethe, Byron, Ibsen: the Faustian idea on stage', *Byron Journal*, 6, 1978, pp. 66-76.

KNIGHT, G. Wilson. 'Byron's dramatic verse', *TLS*, 20 February 1959, p. 97.

KLEIN, John W. 'Byron's neglected plays', *Drama*, 63, Winter, 1961 pp. 34-36.

KUSHWAHA, M. S. 'Byron the dramatist: a reappraisal', *Punjab University Research Bulletin (Arts)*, 3, no. 2, 1972, pp. 113-120.

LIM, Paulino M., Jr. *The style of Lord Byron's plays*. Salzburg: University of Salzburg, 1973. [Salzburg studies in English: Poetic Drama Series, no. 3.]

LINNEY, Romulus. *Childe Harold: a play in two acts*. New York: Dramatists Play Service, 1981.

LUKE, K. McCormick. 'Lord Byron's "Manfred": a study of alienation from within', *University of Toronto Quarterly*, 40, Fall 1970, pp. 15-26.

McGANN, Jerome J. 'Byronic drama in two Venetian plays', *Modern Philology*, LXVI, August 1968, pp. 30-44.

McGANN, Jerome J. 'Staging Byron's "Cain" ', *Keats-Shelley Memorial Bulletin*, XIX, 1968, pp. 24-27.

McVEIGH, Daniel M. ' "In Caines Cynne": Byron and the Mark of Cain', *Modern Language Quarterly*, 43, December 1982, pp. 337-351.

McVEIGH, Daniel M. 'Manfred's curse', *Studies in English Literature*, 22, Autumn 1982, pp. 601-612.

MAGARSHACK, David. *Stanislavsky: a life.* London: MacGibbon & Kee; New York: Chanticleer, 1950. [Stanislavsky's production of *Cain* pp. 353-354].

MANNING, Peter J. 'Edmund Kean and Byron's plays', *Keats-Shelley Journal*, 21-22, 1972-1973, pp. 188-206.

MARTIN, Philip W. *Byron: a poet before his public.* Cambridge: Cambridge University Press, 1982.

MIESEL, Martin. 'The material sublime: John Martin, Byron, Turner and the theatre,' in *Images of Romanticism: verbal and visual affinities*, ed. by Karl Kroeber and William Walling. New Haven: Yale University Press, 1978, pp. 211-232.

MERCHANT, W. Moelwyn. *Creed and Drama: an essay in religious drama.* London: S.P.C.K., 1965.

MOGAN, Joseph J. Jr. 'Pierre and Manfred: Melville's study of the Byronic hero', *Papers on English Language & Literature*, I, Summer 1965, pp. 230-240.

MICHAELS, Leonard. 'Byron's Cain', *PMLA*, LXXXIV, January 1969, pp. 71-78.

MORTENSON, Robert. '*Abel: a mystery* by Philip Dixon Hardy; an answer to Lord Byron's *Cain: a mystery*', *Keats-Shelley Memorial Bulletin*, XIX, 1968, pp. 28-32.

MORTENSON, Robert. 'Byroniana: "Remarks on *Cain*" identified', *Harvard Library Bulletin*, XVI, July 1968, pp. 237-241.

MORTENSON, Robert. 'The copyright of Byron's *Cain*', *Papers of the Bibliographical Society of America*, LXIII, January-March 1969, pp. 5-13.

MUKOYAMA, Yasuko. 'The characters of Byron's *Sardanapalus*', *Journal of Aoyama Gakuin Woman's Junior College* (Tokyo), 11, June 1959, pp. 1-20.

MUKOYAMA, Yasuko. 'The historical background of Byron's *Sardanapalus*', *Journal of Aoyama Gakuin Woman's Junior College*, 8, November 1957, pp. 1-12.

MURRAY, Christopher. *Robert William Elliston, manager: a theatrical biography.* London: Society for Theatre Research, 1975.

NORMAN, Arthur M. Z. 'Dialogue in Byron's dramas', *Notes & Queries*, CXCIX, July 1954, pp. 304-306.

OPPEL, Horst. 'George Gordon Lord Byron: *Sardanapalus*', in *Das englische Drama im 18. und 19. Jahrhundert*, ed. by H. Kosok. Berlin: Erich Schmidt, 1976, pp. 170-183.

PALFFY, Istvan. 'Byron and his dramatic self-portraits.' *Angol Filologiai Tanulmanyok: Hungarian Studies in English*, 11, 1977, pp. 65-72.

PROCHAZKA, Martin. ' "The strangest nourishment for his hypochondriac humour": the expression of the subject in Byron's *Manfred* and Goethe's *Faust*', *Philologica Pragensia*, 25, 3, 1982, pp. 97-109.

PROTOHRISTOVA, Kleo. 'Bajron i negovijat "Manfred" [Byron and his "Manfred"]', *Rodna rec* (Sofia), 3, 1978, pp. 47-52.

QUINLAN, Maurice J. 'Byron's Manfred and Zoroastrianism', *Journal of English and Germanic Philology*, LVII, October 1958, pp. 726-738.

RADCLIFF-UMSTEAD, Douglas. 'Cainism and Gerard de Nerval', *Philological Quarterly*, XLV, April 1966, pp. 395-408.

REISNER, Thomas A. '*Cain*: two romantic interpretations', *Culture*, 31, June 1970, pp. 124-143.

ROBINSON, Charles E. 'The Devil as Doppelgänger in "The Deformed transformed": the sources and meaning of Byron's unfinished drama', *Bulletin of the New York Public Library*, 74, March 1970, pp. 177-202.

RUDDICK, William. 'Lord Byron's historical tragedies', in *Essays on nineteenth century British theatre: the Proceedings of a symposium sponsored by Manchester University, Dept. of Drama*, ed. by Kenneth Richards and Peter Thomson, London: Methuen, 1971, pp. 83-94.

SAINZ de ROBLES, Frederico C. 'Byron y su trio de damas', *Vanguardia espanola* (Barcelona), 3 December, 1971.

SCHIRMER-INHOFF, Ruth. 'Faust in England: ein Bericht', *Anglia*, LXX, no. 2, 1951, pp. 150-185. [On Manfred, pp. 160-162.]

SCOTT, Noel. 'Byron and the stage', *Quarterly Review*, CCXCIV, October, 1955, pp. 496-503.

SHIPLEY, Joseph T. *Guide to great plays*. Washington: Public Affairs Press, 1956. [Includes Byron's *Cain* and Shelley's *Cenci*.]

SIDERIS, Jean. *Historia tou neou Hellenikou theatrou, 1794-1944*, Vol. I: 1794-1908. Athens: Ikaros, 1951. [Discusses Byron's influence in the theatre of Greece.]

SKERRY, Philip J. 'Concentric structures in *Marino Faliero*', *Keats-Shelley Journal*, 32, 1983, pp. 81-107.

SPECTOR, Jack J. *Delacroix: the Death of Sardanapalus*. London: Allen Lane; New York: Viking, 1974.

SPENCE, G. W. 'The moral ambiguity of *Marino Faliero*', *Journal of Australasian Universities Language and Literature Association*, 41, May 1974, pp. 6-17.

SPERRY, Stuart M. 'Byron and the meaning of *Manfred*', *Criticism*, 16, Summer 1974, pp. 189-202.

STEAD, William Force. 'Byron and Keats', *Times Literary Supplement*, 17 June 1960, p. 385.

STEFFAN. T. G. 'Byron's dramas: three untraced MSS', *Book Collector*, XIV, Autumn 1965, p. 367.

STEINER, George. 'At the Turner exhibition', *Encounter*, 44, no. 4, April 1975, pp. 57-62.

STEVENS, H. R. 'Theme and structure in Byron's *Manfred*: the Biblical basis', *Unisa English Studies*, 11, no. 2, 1973, pp. 15-22.

STRIKER, Ardelle. '*Manfred* in concert: an American premiere', *Bulletin of Research in the Humanities*: New York Public Library, 85, Winter 1982, pp. 479-488.

STRINGHAM, Scott. '*I due Foscari*: from Byron's play to Verdi's opera', *West Virginia University Philological Papers*, 17, June 1970, pp. 31-40.

TABORSKI, Boleslaw. *Byron and the theatre*, Salzburg: University of Salzburg, 1972. [Salzburg Studies in English: Poetic Drama, no. 1].

TANDON, B. G. *The imagery of Lord Byron's plays*. Salzburg: University of Salzburg, 1976, [Salzburg Studies in English; Poetic Drama & Poetic Theory, no. 31.]

THOMPSON, Paula. 'The search for equilibrium: Manfred and Macbeth', *Bulletin of the West Virginia Association of College English Teachers* (Huntington, W.Va.), 5, nos. 1-2, 1979, pp. 47-57.

THOMSON, P.W. 'Byron and Edmund Kean — a comment'. *Theatre Research/Recherches Theatrales*, VIII, no. 1, 1966, pp. 17-19.

TIGHE, F. C. 'Byron and Keats', *Times Literary Supplement*, 24 June 1960, p. 401.

TREWIN, J. C. *Mr Macready: a nineteenth century tragedian and his theatre*, London: Harrap, 1955.

TREWIN, J. C. 'Without meeting Byron', *Illustrated London News*, CCI, 8 November 1952, p. 780.

VALDES, Mario J. and Maria Elena de VALDES. *An Unamuno source book: a catalogue of readings and acquisitions, with an introductory essay on Unamuno's dialectical enquiry*. Toronto: University

of Toronto, 1973. [Notes his debt to Byron's *Cain*.]
VANDERBEETS, Richard. 'A note on dramatic necessity and the incest motif in *Manfred*', *Notes & Queries*, CCIX, January 1964, pp.26-28.
VOGEL, Albert. 'Aanteleningen bij Byron's *Manfred*', *Kunst en Kunstleven*, April 1949, pp. 12-13.
WATKINS, Daniel P. 'Violence, class consciousness and ideology in Byron's history plays', *Journal of English Literary History*, 48, Winter 1981, pp. 799-816.
WEINSTOCK, Herbert. *Donizetti and the world of opera in Italy, Paris, and Vienna in the first half of the nineteenth century*. New York: Pantheon, 1963.
WHITLA, William. 'Sources for Browning in Byron, Blake and Poe', *Studies in Browning and his Circle*, 2, Spring 1974, pp. 7-16.
WHITMORE, Allen Perry. *The major characters of Lord Byron's dramas*. Salzburg: University of Salzburg, 1974. [Salzburg Studies in English; Poetic Drama and Poetic Theory Series, no. 6.]
WORMHOUDT, Arthur. 'The five layer structure of sublimation and literary analysis', *American Imago*, XIII, Summer 1956, pp. 205-219.

SAMUEL TAYLOR COLERIDGE
FOX, Arnold B. 'Political and biographical background of Coleridge's "Osorio" ', *Journal of English and Germanic Philology*, LXI, 1962, pp. 258-267.
MOORE, John David. 'Coleridge and the "Modern Jacobinical drama": *Osorio, Remorse* and the development of Coleridge's critique of the stage, 1979-1816', *Bulletin of Research in the Humanities*, 85, 1982; pub. 1984, pp. 443-464.
PRIESTMAN, Donald G. 'Godwin, Schiller and the polemics of Coleridge's *Osorio*', *Bulletin of Research in the Humanities*, 82, 1979, pp. 236-248.
WOODRING, Carl R. 'Two prompt copies of Coleridge's "Remorse" ', *Bulletin of the New York Public Library*, LXV, 1961, pp. 229-235.

JOHN KEATS
BEAUDRY, Harry R. *The English theatre and John Keats*. Salzburg: University of Salzburg, 1973. [Salzburg Studies in English:

Poetic Drama Series, no. 13].
GAL, Istvan. 'Keats's "Prince of Hungary" identified', *The New Hungarian Quarterly*, no. 37, n.d.
GREEN, David B. 'Keats and Schiller', *Modern Language Notes*, LXVI, December 1951, pp. 537-540.
HEWLETT, Dorothy. '*Otho the Great*', *Keats-Shelley Memorial Bulletin*, no. IV, 1952. p. 1.
KEATS, John. 'Manuscripts IV: *Otho the Great* by John Keats', *Library Chronicle* (Texas), 4, February 1972, pp. 58-59.
RZEPKA, Charles J. 'Theatrum mundi and Keats' *Otho the Great*: the self in "Society" ', *Romanticism Past & Present*, 8, no. 1, 1984, pp. 35-50.
SLOTE, Bernice. 'The poet and the poem', *Prairie Schooner*, 55, Spring-Summer 1981, pp. 91-98.

PERCY BYSSHE SHELLEY

ADAMS, Charles L. 'The structure of the Cenci', *Drama Survey*, IV, 1965, pp. 139-147.
ARTAUD, Antonin. *The Cenci*; translated by Simon Watson Taylor. New York: Grove, 1969. [Largely based on Shelley's play.]
BASKYAR, D. D. 'Beatrice of Shelley's drama *The Cenci*', *Indian Journal of English Studies*, 12, 1971, pp. 33-41.
BARZUN, Ernest S. *A study of Shelley's drama, 'The Cenci'*. Folcroft, PA.: Folcroft, 1973. [Reprint of 1908 edition.]
BEBBINGTON, W. G. 'Shelley and the Windsor stage, 1815', *Notes & Queries*, CCI, May 1956, pp. 215-216.
BROPHY, Robert J. ' "Tamar", "The Cenci", and incest'. *American Literature*, 42, May 1970, pp. 241-244.
CAVE, Richard Allen. '*The Cenci* in performance', *Keats-Shelley Memorial Bulletin*, no. XXXVI, 1985, pp. 114-118.
CHAI, Leon. 'Melville and Shelley: speculations on metaphysics, morals, and poetics in "Pierre" and "Shelley's Vision" ', *Emerson Society Quarterly*, 29, no. 1, 1983, pp. 31-45.
CURRAN, Stuart. *Shelley's 'Cenci': scorpions ringed with fire*. Princeton: Princeton University, 1970.
DELMAR, P. Jay. 'Evil and character in Shelley's "The Cenci" ', *Massachusetts Studies in English*, 6, nos. 1-2, 1977, pp. 37-48.
DUERKSON, Roland A. 'The double image of Beatrice Cenci in "The Marble Faun" ', *Michigan Academician*, 1, Spring 1969, pp. 47-55.

ELLIOT, John R., Jr. ' "Feeling hot": Victorian drama and the Censors', *Victorian Newsletter*, 49, Spring 1976, pp. 5-9.
FINDLATER, Richard. *Banned! A review of theatrical censorship in Britain*. London: MacGibbon & Kee, 1967.
FORMAN, Elsa. 'Beatrice Cenci and Alma Murray', *Keats-Shelley Memorial Bulletin*, V, 1953, pp. 5-10.
GERSHMAN, Herbert S. 'Romanticism revisited', *Symposium*, 22, Fall-Winter 1969, pp. 241-254.
GOTTLIEB, Erika. 'Cosmic allegory in "The Cenci" ', *Aligarh Journal of English Studies*, 3, 1978, pp. 24-43.
HICKS, Arthur C. and R. Milton CLARKE. *A stage version of Shelley's 'The Cenci'*. Caldwell, Idaho: The Caxton Printers, 1945.
HOOD, Sharon. 'Note 381. Shelley's "The Cenci" ', *Book Collector*, 24, no. 2, Summer 1975, p. 291.
JOHNSON, Betty F. 'Shelley's "Cenci" and "Mrs Warren's Profession" ', *Shaw Review*, 15, January 1972, pp. 26-34.
LEMONCELLI, Ronald L. 'Cenci as corrupt dramatic poet', *English Language Notes*, 16, December 1978, pp. 103-117.
LESSENICH, Rolf P. 'Godwin and Shelley: rhetoric versus revolution', *Studia Neophologica*, 47, no. 1, 1975, pp. 40-52.
MARCHI, Giovanni. 'La tragedia dei Cenci nelle opere teatrali', *Nuova Antologia*, DIII, August 1968, pp. 530-547.
MARSHALL, William H. ' "Caleb Williams" and "The Cenci" ', *Notes & Queries*, CCV, July 1960, pp. 260-263.
MILLER, Sara Mason. 'Irony in Shelley "The Cenci" ', *University of Mississippi Studies in English*, IX, 1968, pp. 23-25.
MILNE, Fred L. 'Shelley's "The Cenci": the ice motif and the ninth circle of Dante's Hell', *Tennessee Studies in Literature*, 22, 1977, pp. 117-132.
MORAVIA, Alberto. 'Beatrice Cenci', *Botteghe Oscure* (Rome), XVI, 1955, pp. 363-461.
OTTEN, Terry. 'Christabel, Beatrice, and the encounter with evil', *Bucknell Review*, XVII, no. 2, May 1969, pp. 19-31.
REES, Joan. 'Shelley's Orsino: evil in "The Cenci" ', *Keats-Shelley Memorial Bulletin*, XII, 1961, pp. 3-6.
RICCI, Corrado. *Beatrice Cenci*; translated by Morris Bishop and Henry Longan Stuart. London: Peter Owen, 1955.
RIEGER, James. 'Shelley's Paterin Beatrice', *Studies in Romanticism*, IV, Spring 1965, pp. 169-184.

SCHAUBERT, Else von. *Shelleys Tragödie 'The Cenci' und Marlowes Doppeldrama 'Tamburlaine'*. Paderborn: Ferdinand Schöningh, 1965.

SCHELL, John F. 'Shelley's "The Cenci": corruption and the calculating faculty', *University of Mississippi Studies in English*, 2, 1981, pp. 1-14.

SHAW, George Bernard. 'Art Corner', *Shaw Review*, 15, January 1972, pp. 35-38.

SHAW, Bernard. *Platform and pulpit*, edited by Dan H. Laurence. London: Hart-Davis, 1962.

SHELLEY, Percy Bysshe. *The Cenci*, edited by Roland A. Duerkson. Indianapolis: Bobbs-Merrill, 1970. [Library of Liberal Arts].

SHELLEY, Percy Bysshe. *The Cenci, a tragedy in five acts, given from the poet's own editions*. Introduction by Alfred Forman and H. Buxton Forman, and a prologue by John Todhunter. New York: Phaeton, 1970. [Reprint of 1886 edition.]

SHELLEY, Percy Bysshe. ' "The Cenci" at the Old Vic', *Keats-Shelley Journal*, IX, Winter 1960, p. 2.

SHELLEY, Percy Bysshe. ' "The Cenci" produced at the University of Chicago', *Keats-Shelley Journal*, VIII, Winter 1959, pp. 10-11.

SHELLEY, Percy Bysshe. *Prologue in Heavan [sic]; the introductory scene from 'Faust'; with translation into English by Percy Bysshe Shelley*. Melbourne, Australia: Truesdell Press, 1949.

SHIMIZU, Isamu. 'Personal views of "The Cenci" ', *Memoris* (Aichi Women's Junior College), III, December 1952, pp. 1-31. [In Japanese.]

STATES, Bert O., Jr. 'Addendum: the stage history of Shelley's "The Cenci" ', *PMLA*, LXXII, September 1957, pp. 633-644.

STATES, Bert O., Jr. ' "The Cenci" as a stage play', *PMLA*, LXXV, March 1960, pp. 148-149.

STATES, Bert O., Jr. 'Standing of the extreme verge in "King Lear" and other high places', *Georgia Review*, 36, 1982, pp. 417-425.

STEINER, Francis G. 'Shelley and Goethe's "Faust" ', *Rivista di letturata moderne*, New series, II, April June, 1951, pp. 269-274.

STEFFAN, Truman Guy. 'Seven accounts of the Cenci and Shelley's drama', *Studies in English Literature*, 9, Autumn 1969, pp. 601-618.

THORN, Arline R. 'Shelley's "The Cenci" as tragedy', *Costerus*, 9, 1973, pp. 219-228.

THORNDIKE, Dame Sybil and Barbara JEFFORD. 'From "the

Cenci" to "Saint Joan" ', *Shavian*, 16, 1959, pp. 24-26.
TURNER, Justin G. ' "The Cenci": Shelley vs the truth', *American Book Collector*, 22, February 1972, pp. 5-9.
TREWIN, J. C. 'The lifted ban', *Illustrated London News*, CCXXXIV, 31 January 1959, p. 180.
TREWIN, J. C. 'Rebellion', *Illustrated London News*, CCXXXIV, 16 May 1959, p. 852.
TWITCHELL, James B. 'Shelley's use of vampirism in "The Cenci" ', *Tennessee Studies in Literature*, 24, 1979, pp. 120-133.
WALBRIDGE, Earle F. 'Drames a clef: a list of plays with characters based on real people', *Bulletin of the New York Public Library*, LX, April 1956, pp. 159-174. [Mentions Shelley's 'Swellfoot the Tyrant'.]
WARNKE, Frank J. 'Poetic drama on European stages', *New Republic*, CXLI, 24 August 1959, pp. 30-31.
WARREN, John W. 'The Cenci Tragedy: heroism restored', *Tennessee Philological Bulletin: Proceedings of the annual meeting of the Tennessee Philological Association*, 9, no. 1, 1972, pp. 3-13.
WATSON, Melvin R. 'Shelley and tragedy: the case of Beatrice Cenci', *Keats-Shelley Journal*, VII, 1958, pp. 13-21.
WHITAKER, A. 'Shelley's Cenci', *Notes & Queries*, CC, November 1955, p. 498.
WHITE, Harry. 'Beatrice Cenci and Shelley's avenger', *Essays in Literature*, Macomb, Ill., 5, 1978, pp. 27-38.
WHITE, Robert L. ' "Rappaccini's daughter", "The Cenci" and the Cenci legend', *Studi Americani*, XLV, 1968, pp. 63-86.
WHITMAN, Robert F. 'Beatrice's pernicious mistake in "The Cenci" ', *PMLA*, LXXIV, June 1959, pp. 249-253.
WILSON, James D. 'Beatrice Cenci and Shelley's vision of moral responsibility', *Ariel: a review of international English literature*, 9, July, 1978, pp. 75-89.
WORTON, Michael. 'Speech and silence in "The Cenci" ', in *Essays on Shelley*, edited by Miriam Allott. Totowa, NJ.: Barnes & Nobles, 1982, pp. 105-124.

WILLIAM WORDSWORTH

BANERJI, Jibon. 'The role of Godwinian ideas in "The Borderers" ', *Calcutta Review*, n.s. 1, January – March 1970, pp. 419-422.
OWEN, W. J. B. ' "The Borderers" and the aesthetics of drama', *Wordsworth Circle*, 6, no. 4, 1975, pp. 227-239.

PIPKIN, James W. ' "The Borderers" and the genesis of Wordsworth's spots of time', *Tennessee Studies in Literature*, 24, 1979.

POLLIN, Burton R. 'Permutations of names in "The Borderers", or hints of Godwin, Charles Lloyd and a real renegade', *Wordsworth Circle*, 4, Winter 1973, pp. 31-35.

PRIESTMAN, Donald G. ' "The Borderers": Wordsworth's addenda to Godwin', *University of Toronto Quarterly*, 44, Fall 1974, pp. 56-65.

STODDARD, Eve Walsh. ' "The Borderers": a critique of both reason and feeling as moral agents', *Wordsworth Circle*, 11, 1980, pp. 93-97.

STORCH, R. F. 'Wordsworth's "The Borderers": the poet as anthropologist', *Journal of English Literary history*, XXXVI, 1969, pp. 340-360.

THORSLEV, Peter L. Jr. 'Wordsworth's "The Borderers" and the romantic villain-hero', *Studies in Romanticism*, Boston University, V, 1966, pp. 84-103.

INDEX

Adelphi Theatre, 81
Aeschylus, 16, 45, 63, 72, 82.
Agate, James, 88, 91.
Alfieri, Vittorio 45, 57, 72, 82, 95. *Mirra*, 57, 72, 82.
Antheil, George, 58.
Aristophanes, 63, 65, 72.
Aristotle, 67-68, 77.
Arnold, Matthew, 62.
Artaud, Antonin, 94-95; *The Cenci*, 94-95
Astley's Amphitheatre, 81.

Baillie, Joanna, 41.
Barton, Anne, 81-82, 111 n.45.
Beaumont, Francis and Fletcher, John, 21; *The Beggar's Bush*, 21; *The Pilgrim*, 21; *Rule a Wife and Have a Wife*, 30.
Beckett, Samuel, 76, 104.
Bene, Carmelo, 53.
Benthall, Michael, 87.
Bernhardt, Sarah, 91.
Blake, William, 13; *Edward the Third*, 13; *An Island in the Moon*, 13; *Poetical Sketches*, 13.
Bloom, Harold, 62.
Bond, Edward, 58-59.
Boucicault, Dion, 99; *The Corsican Brothers*, 99.
Boydell Shakespeare Gallery, The, 36-37.
Brecht, Bertolt, 82, 88, 104; *The Caucasian Chalk Circle*, 88.
Bristol Old Vic Studio Theatre, 72, 87, 89, 93.
Brown, Charles, 18.
Browning, Robert, 61, 62; *The Ring and the Book*, 62.
Bunn, Alfred, 79, 99.
Burke, Edmund, 14; *Reflections on the Revolution in France*, 14.
Byron, Lord George Gordon, 9, 10, 12, 13, 15-16, 21, 23, 27-28, 30, 37, 39-46, 47-60, 61, 65, 66, 72, 73, 76, 79-83, 86, 95-104, 111 n.45; *An Address to Drury Lane Theatre*, 39-40; *Beppo*, 49, 55-56, 58; *Cain*, 12, 16, 51, 58, 65; *Childe Harold's Pilgrimage*, 12, 49; *The Corsair*, 55; *The Deformed Transformed*, 16, 59-60, 65; *Don Juan*, 49, 110 n.7; *The Giaour*, 55, 95; *Heaven and Earth*, 16, 51-52, 55, 65; *The Lament of Tasso*, 49; *Lara*, 55, 95; *Manfred*, 12, 15-16, 47, 49-50, 51-52, 53-56, 65, 71, 79-81, 99, 110 n.7, 110 n.8; *Marino Faliero*, 16, 43, 45-46, 50-51, 53, 71, 72, 81, 82, 95, 96, 98, 100-102, 103, 111 n.45, 112 n.59, 112 n.67; *Mazeppa*, 81; *The Prophecy of Dante*, 49; *Sardanapalus*, 16, 48, 51, 65, 71, 81-82, 96, 98, 99-100, 112 n.63; *The Two Foscari*, 16, 45, 48, 51, 53, 71, 96, 98, 102-104; *Werner*, 16, 43, 52-53, 81, 96, 97-98, 99, 100, 111 n.55, 112 n.61.

Calderón de la Barca, 17, 64, 65, 68, 69, 73, 82; *El Mágico prodigioso*, 17, 65; *La Vida es sueño*, 69.
Caroline, Queen, Consort to George IV, 17, 65.
Casson, Lewis, 87.
Chekov, Anton, 104.
Cibber, Colley, 25.
Coëllo, Antonio, 22.
Cole, J. W., 100.
Coleridge, Samuel Taylor, 9, 11, 12, 13, 14-15, 18-23, 26, 27, 28, 29-30, 31, 36, 37, 38, 42, 61, 70, 72, 81, 84-86, 87, 104; *Biographia Literaria*, 27; *Christabel*, 84; *The Death of Wallenstein*, 14; *Diadeste, the Arabia Rite*, 22; *The Fall of Robespierre*, 14; *Kubla Khan*, 84; *Laugh Till You Love Him*, 22; *Osorio*, 84; *The Piccolomini*, 14-15; *Remorse*, 14-15, 17, 19, 20, 22, 81, 84-86; *The Rime of the Ancient Mariner*, 84; *Sibylline Leaves*, 22; *The Triumph of Loyalty*, 22; *Zapolya*, 15, 20, 27.
Coleridge, Sara, 18-19.
Colman, George, the elder, 25.
Colman, George, the younger, 29, 38;

Blue Beard, 38.
Cooke, George Frederick, 29, 82.
Cooke, Thomas Potter, 81.
Covent Garden Theatre, 13, 15, 17, 18, 26, 34, 38, 39, 79.

Dante Alighieri, 67.
Dawson, Paul, 66.
Dibdin, Charles, 15, 29.
Dickens, Charles, 19, 98; *The Old Curiosity Shop*, 88.
Drury Lane Theatre, 9, 14, 15, 16, 18, 21, 22, 26, 27, 34, 39, 40, 42, 43, 45, 47, 48, 49, 51, 72, 79, 81, 84, 85, 86, 95.

Edinburgh Review, The, 100.
Egan Pierce, 81; *Life in London*, 81.
Elliston, Robert, 39, 85, 95-96, 111 n.45.
Euripides, 17, 45, 63, 64, 72, 89; *The Bacchae*, 89; *The Cyclops*, 17, 63, 64.

Farquharson, Robert, 88.

Garrick, David, 25, 41, 48, 73.
George IV, King of England, 17.
Gifford, William, 84.
Gisborne, Maria, 63, 64.
Godwin, William, 11, 17.
Goethe, Johann Wolfgang von, 16, 17, 20, 56, 59, 65, 110 n.7; *Faust*, 16, 17, 56, 59, 65.
Goldoni, Carlo, 28.
Grand Theatre, Islington, 87.
Griffith, Hugh, 88-89.

Hack, Keith, 100-102, 103, 112 n.67.
Hallam, Arthur Henry, 62.
Hazlitt, William, 9, 11, 12, 13, 21, 22, 31, 35, 36, 37, 95.
Hobhouse, John Cam, 79.
Hogarth, William, 34.
Holcroft, Thomas, 17, 84.
Holland, Henry, 34.
Hoyland, William, 89, 93.
Hunt, James Henry Leigh, 28-29, 32-33, 38-39, 40, 52, 64, 72; *Critical Essays on the Performers of the London Theatre*, 28; *The Descent of Liberty*, 64; *The Examiner*, 28, 38-39; *The Liberal*, 52; *The Reflector*, 28.
Hurd, Richard, 62.

Ibsen, Henrik, 104.
Irving, Sir Henry, 88, 100.

James I, King of England, 70.
Jefford, Barbara, 92-93, 111 n.37.
Jeffrey, Lord Francis, 100.
Jerrold, Douglas, 81; *Black-Eyed Susan*, 81.
Johnson, Dr. Samuel, 26.
Joyce, James, 57-58; *Finnegans Wake*, 57; *A Portrait of the Artist as a Young Man*, 57-58; *Ulysses*, 57.

Kalidasa, 65; *Sakuntala*, 65.
Kean, Charles, 99-100, 112 n.62.
Kean, Edmund, 18, 21, 23-24, 26, 37-39, 41, 63, 73, 79, 82, 86, 96.
Keats, John, 13, 18, 23-24, 45, 61, 62; *King Stephen*, 18; *Otho the Great*, 18.
Kelly, Michael, 96.
Kemble, John Philip, 22, 24, 25, 37-39, 82, 84.
Knight, G. Wilson, 12.
Kotzebue, August von, 28.

Lamb, Charles, 35, 36-37, 38, 48; *Specimens of English Dramatic Poets*, 48.
Layard, Sir Austen Henry, 99.
Lee, Harriet, 16.
Leopardi, Giacomo, 73.
Lewes, George Henry, 98, 99, 112 n.62, 112 n.63.
Lewis, Matthew Gregory, 59; *The Wood Demon*, 59.
Lloyd, Charles, 72.
Lockhart, John Gibson, 95.
Lyceum Theatre, The, 100.

Machiavelli, Niccolo, 25.
Macready, William Charles, 25, 81, 82, 96-99, 100, 111 n.55, 112 n.59, 112 n.61, 112 n.63, 112 n.67.
Maeterlinck, Maurice, 104.
Man-Fred, 80.
Marlowe, Christopher, 15, 54, 56; *The Tragedy of Dr. Faustus*, 15, 54, 56.
Marchand, Leslie, A., 95.
Marston, John Westland, 79, 80, 96-98, 99, 100.
Martin, John, 79.
Mathews, Charles, 29.
Maturin, Charles Robert, 26, 44, 95; *Bertram*, 26, 27, 95, 111 n.43; *Melmoth the Wanderer*, 26.
Maurois, André, 70.
Medwin, Thomas, 42, 45, 46, 82; *Conversations of Lord Byron*, 82.

Index

Mellinger, Leonie, 93-94.
Menken, Adah Isaacs, 81.
Mill, John Stuart, 62.
Milman, Henry Hart, 26, 27; *Fazio*, 26, 27.
Milner, H. M., 81; *Mazeppa*, 81.
Milton, John, 67.
Moncrieff, William (George) Thomas, 81; *Tom and Jerry*, 81.
Moore, Thomas, 55; *The Loves of the Angels*, 55.
Mozart, Wolfgang Amadeus, 16; *Don Giovanni*, 16.
Murray, Alma, 90-91.
Murray, John, 43, 47, 50, 54-55, 57, 82.

New Theatre, The, 87.
Newman, Cardinal John Henry, 58.

Old Vic Theatre, The, 87, 92.
O'Neill, Eliza, 17, 26, 63, 72, 79, 82.
Otway, Thomas, 50, 72; *Venice Preserved*, 50, 72.

Paine, Thomas, 14.
Peacock, Thomas Love, 17, 26, 30, 63, 67, 79; *Memoirs of Percy Bysshe Shelley*, 30.
Phelps, Samuel, 112 n.61.
Pickersgill, Joshua, 16.
Pinter, Harold, 104.
Pirandello, Luigi, 71; *Enrico Quattro*, 71; *Sei Personaggi in cerca d'autore*, 71.
Plato, 63, 64, 72; *Symposium*, 63, 64.
Pocock, Isaac, 81; *The Miller and His Men*, 81.
Pope, Alexander, 42.
Praz, Mario, 53.

Racine, Jean, 45, 72, 103; *Andromaque*, 72, 73, 103, 112 n.71; *Bérénice*, 103, 112 n.71; *Britannicus*, 103, 112, n.71; *Phèdre*, 72, 73.
Rae, Alexander, 85.
Reynolds, Frederick, 29.
Robinson, Henry Crabb, 19, 20, 79, 90, 99, 110 n.7, 110 n.8, 112 n.63.
Rowlandson, Thomas, 34.

Schiller, Johann Christoph Friedrich von, 14; *The Death of Wallenstein*, 14; *Cabal and Love* 14; *The Piccolomini*, 14; *The Robbers*, 14.
Schlegel, August Wilhelm von, 25;

Lectures on Dramatic Literature, 25.
Schumann, Robert, 53; *Manfred*, 53.
Scott, Sir Walter, 34-35, 36, 42; *Essay on the Drama*, 34-35.
Sgricci, Tommaso, 66.
Shakespeare, William, 11, 12, 18, 20-21, 23-24, 25-27, 30, 35-37, 38, 42, 44, 45, 47, 48, 56, 67, 82; *Antony and Cleopatra*, 56; *Coriolanus*, 82; *Cymbeline*, 92; *Hamlet*, 88; *Henry IV*, 88; *Henry VI*, 14; *King Lear*, 14, 25, 31, 32, 48, 56; *Macbeth*, 26, 35-36, 38, 92, 102, 111 n.38; *The Merchant of Venice*, 96; *A Midsummer Night's Dream*, 9, 35; *Othello*, 14, 23-24, 66, 83, 96; *Richard II*, 14, 20, 21; *Richard III*, 25, 37, 40, 96; *The Tempest*, 35, 70; *Twelfth Night*, 92; *The Winter's Tale*, 15.
Shaw, George Bernard, 16, 91; *Saint Joan*, 91-92.
Shelley, Mary, 17, 26, 63, 65, 66; *Proserpine, a Mythological Drama*, 65, 66.
Shelley, Percy Bysshe, 9, 13, 16-18, 24-25, 26-27, 30-32, 39, 45, 61-77, 79, 82, 86-95, 104; *Adonais*, 27; *The Cenci*, 16-17, 45, 62, 63, 64, 67, 71, 72, 73, 75-76, 79, 86-95, 103; *Charles the First*, 17, 31-32, 63, 65, 68-71, 73, 74, 75; *A Defence of Poetry*, 24-25, 31, 39, 66-68, 72; 'Fragments of an Unfinished Drama', 17; *Hellas*, 16, 65, 66, 71, 74-75, 77; *Julian and Maddalo*, 18, 64; *The Mask of Anarchy*, 64, 68; *Oedipus Tyrannus or Swellfoot the Tyrant*, 17, 65; *Prometheus Unbound*, 16, 63, 64, 71, 73, 74, 76; *Rosalind and Helen*, 64; *The Triumph of Life*, 77.
Shelley Society, The, 87.
Sheridan, Richard Brinsley, 14, 27-28, 29, 84; *Pizarro*, 28; *The School for Scandal*, 30.
Sherwell, Debbie, 93-94, 103.
Siddons, Mrs. Sarah, 22, 37-39, 82, 96.
Sophocles, 45, 67.
Southey, Robert, 14, 19, 61, 70, 84, 86.
Spenser, Edmund, 45.
Strand Theatre, The, 80.
Strindberg, August, 104.
Sullivan, John, 58.
Surrey Theatre, The Royal Circus and, 15, 26.

Tasso, Torquato, 17-18, 27, 67; *Discorsi del Poema Eroico*, 67.
Tate, Nahum, 25.

Tennyson, Lord Alfred, 58, 61, 62.
Terry, Ellen, 100.
Thorndike, Sybil, 87, 91-92, 93, 95.
Times, The, 87, 90, 92-93, 102.
Tree, Ellen, 80.
Trelawny, Edward John, 65, 66.

Verdi, Giuseppe, 53; *Marino Faliero*, 53; *The Two Foscari*, 53.
Vezin, Hermann, 87-88.

Wagner, Richard, 16; *The Ring of the Nibelungs*, 16.
Wilde, Oscar, 88; *Salomé*, 88.
Williams, Edward, 65; *The Promise*, 65.

Williams, Jane, 65.
Wilmot, Mrs. 41; *Ina*, 41.
Winston, James, 96.
Wordsworth, Dorothy, 13.
Wordsworth, William, 9, 10, 11, 12, 13, 31, 61, 70, 72, 83-84, 86; *The Borderers*, 12, 13, 83-84; *Lyrical Ballads*, 84; *The Prelude*, 11-12; 'Resolution and Independence', 11; 'The Thorn', 11.
Wroughton, Richard, 21.

Yeats, William Butler, 9, 10, 11, 13, 28, 56, 82, 86, 104.
Young Vic Studio Theatre, 100-101.